DON'T BURN THIS
COUNTRY

DON'T BURN THIS COUNTRY

SURVIVING AND THRIVING
IN OUR WOKE DYSTOPIA

DAVE RUBIN

SENTINEL

Sentinel
An imprint of Penguin Random House LLC
penguinrandomhouse.com

Copyright © 2022 by Emma Dog Productions, LLC

Penguin supports copyright. Copyright fuels creativity, encourages diverse voices, promotes
free speech, and creates a vibrant culture. Thank you for buying an authorized
edition of this book and for complying with copyright laws by not reproducing, scanning,
or distributing any part of it in any form without permission. You are supporting writers
and allowing Penguin to continue to publish books for every reader.

Most Sentinel books are available at a discount when purchased in quantity for sales
promotions or corporate use. Special editions, which include personalized covers, excerpts,
and corporate imprints, can be created when purchased in large quantities. For more
information, please call (212) 572-2232 or email specialmarkets@penguinrandomhouse.com.
Your local bookstore can also assist with discounted bulk purchases using the Penguin
Random House corporate Business-to-Business program. For assistance in locating a
participating retailer, e-mail B2B@penguinrandomhouse.com.

Library of Congress Cataloging-in-Publication Data

Names: Rubin, Dave, 1976– author.
Title: Don't burn this country: surviving and thriving in our woke dystopia / Dave Rubin.
Description: [New York] : Sentinel, [2022] | Includes bibliographical references and index.
Identifiers: LCCN 2021047001 (print) | LCCN 2021047002 (ebook) |
ISBN 9780593332146 (hardcover) | ISBN 9780593332153 (ebook)
Subjects: LCSH: Liberty. | Individualism—United States. |
Liberalism—United States. | United States—Politics and government—2017–2021. |
United States—Social conditions—2020–
Classification: LCC JC599.U5 R75 2022 (print) | LCC JC599.U5 (ebook) |
DDC 323.44—dc23/eng/20220206
LC record available at https://lccn.loc.gov/2021047001
LC ebook record available at https://lccn.loc.gov/2021047002

Printed in the United States of America
1st Printing

To David

(Not me, the other one.)

Contents

Introduction:
Welcome to Dystopia

Like most Americans, I woke up on March 15, 2020, wondering if I should wash an unopened box of Ziploc bags. It was the beginning of a national lockdown. Restaurants, bars, small mom-and-pop shops were being shuttered. Aisles in big box stores lay barren—no cleaning supplies, no toilet paper, no bread, no water. Last-minute impulse buys at the checkout counter like packs of gum or tabloid magazines had been replaced by ransacked cardboard cartons reserved for light-blue PPE face masks and little bottles of hand sanitizer.

The NBA season announced suspension, schools closed, ships dropped their anchors, travel bans were enforced, and curfews were put into place. There was something viscerally exciting about it all—like when a thunderstorm causes the electricity to go out or when a nasty blizzard makes for a snow day. It'll only be for two weeks, they say. "Two weeks to flatten the curve."

Rushing to prepare for two weeks indoors, I planned to pop into CVS to pick up a few last-minute things and then head home. As I pulled into the parking lot, I remembered that just around the corner was a dog shelter. Only a month before, our beloved dog, Emma, passed away, but *nowhere* in the plan was getting another dog. It was supposed to be a busy year—my first book tour was on the horizon and my company Locals had just launched. There was way too much travel on my agenda to justify getting a new dog. What's more, my husband, David, made me promise we wouldn't even think about getting another dog before the fall.

I grabbed my items, checked out, got into my car, and made my way toward the local shelter, just to see who the new arrivals were, knowing we weren't going to be making an adoption. I figured there'd be no harm in saying hello to a few dogs and scratching a few bellies before locking myself in my house for two whole weeks.

Inside the shelter, it was totally empty besides the howling dogs and faceless, mask-wearing workers. Ominous to say the least. They'd rescued five dogs that morning from a Los Angeles kill shelter, one of which was a white and honey-colored pit bull mix with a bald spot on his head. Something about him reminded me of Emma. He sat there quietly and nervously—his big round eyes piercing mine, his tail anxiously wagging. A worker showed me some paperwork from the previous shelter with a time stamp on it: 3:15 p.m., March 15, 2020—his scheduled euthanasia.

My stomach churned and my phone buzzed. It was David. I left the shelter and answered my phone.

David and I had been having ongoing conversations about starting a family (as *actual* dads, not just dog dads). He had always wanted kids. I was always on the fence. No, wait, I take that back. I *never* wanted kids—I thought being gay was an easy out. Kids, I had always thought, wouldn't be compatible with my career and, well, doing whatever I wanted to do whenever I wanted to do it. So, while David and I would continue having conversations and meeting with fertility doctors, we kept punting the reality further down the road. But there I was: forty-three years old and the world was ending. Something shifted in me—I felt like it was now or never. If the world was really ending, I decided that creating life was my only chance at saving it.

I rushed home and we called our fertility doctor.

Doc's response? "We're closing in two hours. You better get here, because I'm not sure when we'll be opening again. If we're able to get an egg and a surrogate but don't have the sperm, then we're at an indefinite standstill."

We hopped into the car and drove at light speed for about twenty-five minutes. The tension on the roads was palpable. People honking and swerving. The 405 freeway was a parking lot (which, to be fair, was normal). On the overpass, we saw bird's-eye views of grocery stores with lines out the door that seemed to stretch on for miles.

We arrived at the clinic and got out of the car. Oddly enough, this street in Brentwood was empty. It was an unusually windy and blustery day, which made everything seem even eerier.

Once we finished at the clinic, after finalizing one of the biggest decisions we'll ever make, we got back into the car and headed toward home. What I knew, but David did not, is that I had no intention of heading home from the sperm bank. No, I was heading back to the animal shelter to go and save that nameless mutt that had not left my mind (except maybe when I was in that little room at the sperm bank).

"So, uh, I thought maybe we'd just swing by that animal shelter to see what's going on?"

"Oh my god, Dave. What have you done?"

"Let's just foster him for a week!" I suggested. After that, I figured, things would be nearly normal again. We walked out of the shelter that day with an unnamed pit bull-boxer mix. You now know him as Clyde.

You know what happened next: the curve never flattened, and nothing went back to normal.

My book tour, travel, *everything* was canceled. People went months without seeing their families, skipping out on Christmases and Thanksgivings even when it could have been their grandparents' last. Those who did see their families were condemned as reckless and irresponsible. ("You're gonna kill Grandma!") The US presidential election came and went, fraught with skepticism, and America's biggest (and sketchiest) pharmaceutical corporations raced to manufacture and distribute a vaccine before it was ever approved or even properly tested. Eventually, cities began to slowly open up and relax mandates again—only to later reinforce even more severe mandates than before.

These never-ending lockdowns had extreme ripple effects. Businesses were boarded up. Political protests erupted in the streets. Sales of firearms reached record highs—five million Americans bought them for the first time in 2020 (myself included).[1]

Finally, people went nuts! Locking themselves indoors for over a year, some occasionally ventured outside their homes to walk their dogs or go for Sunday drives, but never without their trusty mask. Suicide is still on the rise—one in four young Americans have considered or attempted it since the beginning of the lockdown.[2] Following federal vaccine mandates, enforced by large corporations, many Americans—including former "frontline workers"—have been forced out of their jobs for refusing the jab.

Now, two years after the initial pandemic panic, we know that our country's leaders—including not only our government but also our media—used COVID-19 as an opportunity to test our limits. They appear to have asked themselves: Just how much oppression will the American people tolerate? Will otherwise healthy people wear a mask any time they leave their homes? Can we pressure them into taking an unproven and untested vaccine? Will they spy on their neighbors to enforce quarantine rules? Can people be guilted into looting and rioting in the streets for a cause they don't understand? The unfortunate truth is that most Americans, it turned out, were happy to submit while our country burned.

It might surprise you, but this book is not a dystopian novel. (If it were, I'd totally cast Chris Pratt as yours truly in the movie adaptation.)

Life these days sure does feel like dystopian fiction, though it's not exactly what George Orwell had in mind. Instead of a colorless society of factory slaves, ours is one in which our government creates problems, blames its people, then manufactures a terrible solution. Think about it. For four years, the Man told us that Trump was an evil orange monster—putting "kids in cages," killing the planet, killing our grandmas—and demonized over half of the American voting population for electing him in. Luckily, they told us, a single vote for Trump's opponent or an injection can "restore normalcy," casting all memory of him away like a spell.

Well, people cast the vote and got the jab, yet "normalcy" never came. The same technological overlords who canceled the former president are now canceling us, "experts" warn that COVID is still a risk, and social unrest never sleeps. As of this writing, in December 2021, our totalitarian nightmare is still ramping up. Kids are wearing masks to school while politicians dine freely with lobbyists. Dr. Seuss has been banned from libraries and replaced with Drag Queen Story hours. We've fired nurses in the name of health. Children as young as five are being indoctrinated with racist ideas. And the mainstream media won't tell us things we can see with our own eyes, like that the leader of the free world has severe cognitive decline. It's almost as if the truth is a time-release capsule.

In 2019, before any of this pandemic chaos, I began writing *Don't Burn This Book*, defending classically liberal values—like tolerance and free self-expression—against the values of today's liberals, who support just the opposite: censorship and mass shame. In essence, *Don't Burn This Book* was my last-ditch effort to save liberals from themselves.

But today, I'm not so sure the original concept of liberalism is salvageable. The problem is we've *overdosed* on tolerance and self-expression to such an extent that we actually don't stand for anything. Many "classical liberals" and so-called Republicans even supported vaccine mandates, claiming that private corporations can enforce whatever rules they like. If you are willing to defend "tolerance" above all else, when will you stand up for the truth?

Over the years, "tolerant" liberals have morphed into a politically correct mafia, and the only reason we were happy to let them rule us is that to question them would've designated us the worst and most unacceptable political affiliation.

No, I'm not talking about Nazis. (Does the word *Nazi* even mean anything anymore?) I mean a word so evil, so nefarious, that it makes hipsters and Hollywood actors freak out even worse than when Whole Foods is out of soy milk: *a conservative.*

Yes, I said it: the *c*-word.

The word that implies some ideas are so bad we cannot tolerate them. The word that suggests that maybe family is a good thing, and that more people should focus on their families instead of on impersonal social causes. The word that demands we not only defend American values as good but also refuse to back down when they're threatened.

For years, I have advocated classically liberal values, and I always will. But as American civilization deteriorates around us, I do not believe free speech, tolerance, and all the rest alone are enough. Right now we must fight to conserve the values our country was founded on: life and liberty.

What we need, and what this book will teach you how to start, is a strong movement dedicated to dismantling and resisting the oppressive woke machine and corrupt Washington oligarchy. A movement that advocates loudly on behalf of individual rights—including the right to challenge the system, the science, and the stories we are spoon-fed by our media. The reason, I believe, many well-meaning people on the cusp of a political breakthrough do not speak up loudly enough about this is that they don't understand just how severe the threats to our individual freedoms really are.

Well folks, it's now or never. And I don't mean that like when a politician says it every four years and then nothing ever changes. I mean it literally. This moment we are in *right now* is genuinely the last chance to defend America from tyranny. Wokeism fueled by media manipulation is the Death Star of our time.

But there's always a way to blow up a Death Star.

DON'T BURN THIS
COUNTRY

1

THERE ARE NO OTHER LETTERS IN "I"

The question isn't who is going to let me; it's who is going to stop me.

Ayn Rand, *The Fountainhead*

The Fight for Individual Rights

As political unrest in the Middle East exploded in the second half of 2021, I noticed a trend online that really knocked me off my chair: a new social justice movement called "Queers for Palestine." The movement, almost exclusively driven by people who live, unsurprisingly, in the US, is pretty straightforward. Gay and/or transgender American hipsters decided they empathize dearly with the oppressed people of Palestine, so they paraded in the streets of cities across the country declaring their solidarity.

All I have to say to these kids is there's no gay pride parade in Gaza. The simple truth is that Queers for Palestine is very different than

Palestine for Queers, which usually ends in a fierce and fabulous trip off a rooftop for a pink-haired, genderqueer nonbinary Latinx lesbian.

Especially since the summer of 2020, ignorant displays of wokeness like these have become insufferable. What's worse, I can guarantee not a single soul who attended a Black Lives Matter rally on the mean streets of Park Slope, Brooklyn, has ever experienced true oppression in their lives. And the fact that the majority of the social justice crowd—woke liberals—does not understand just how lucky they are is very, very dangerous.

Yeonmi Park would know this better than anyone. Park was born in the northern part of North Korea in 1993. Growing up, she would regularly go without food and was made to believe that Kim Jong Il could read her mind. Her father risked everything to provide for his wife and two young daughters, but he was later imprisoned and tortured by the regime for trading on the black market.

When Yeonmi was thirteen, the Park family faced a difficult reality: die of starvation or die trying to be free. They chose the latter. Weighing sixty pounds and having just undergone a botched appendectomy, she crossed the Chinese border and waded through the icy Yalu River guided by human traffickers.

The moment they successfully escaped North Korea, they became sex slaves in China. Her mother was bought for sixty-five dollars. Yeonmi was bought for two hundred. She tried to kill herself, but one of the traffickers took a sick form of pity on her and said that if she became his mistress, that he would buy her mother and bring the family back together.

While in China, Yeonmi learned that she could be free in South Korea. So with seven others and armed only with a compass and the

North Star, she escaped her captor and walked across the freezing Gobi Desert to Mongolia, and was eventually caught by a Mongolian soldier. Defectors carry poison with them in case they are caught and sent back to North Korea. As she reached for the poison to end her life, the soldier sympathized and contacted South Korea instead of North Korea.

During our conversation on *The Rubin Report*, I asked Yeonmi if life in China was better than her life in North Korea. She responded, "At thirteen, somehow I learned not to feel. It wasn't like I was thinking, *Am I happy here?* It was that every second was survival."

In South Korea, she learned that thinking for herself took a lot of effort. Instead of being told what to wear, what to listen to, or what to watch, she suddenly had to decide on her own. Despite the freedoms and quality of life being drastically better, Yeonmi felt a deep loneliness setting in, as no one seemed to understand her plight and most South Koreans looked down on North Korean defectors.

Years later, she moved to America—"the land of the free and the home of the brave." She was excited for the new life that awaited her, far away from the totalitarianism of her homeland and the loneliness of South Korea. One day, at around 2 p.m., Yeonmi was walking down Michigan Avenue in Chicago when three women forcefully stole her wallet. When she tried to grab hold of her attackers, they punched her in the face, stole her purse, and held her down as the one with the bag ran away.

As she yelled, begging for help, the surrounding Chicagoans told her to stop yelling—that she was being racist. The three women who attacked her happened to be black.

This was a strange moment for Yeonmi. This was not what she had expected from America. Worse than that, it felt oddly familiar. She knew this feeling of being silenced—of not being able to ask for help—more than anyone. She said, "What I see in America is that when I was born in North Korea, I was the third generation of this oppression. I didn't even know what the alternative was like. But my grandmother knew. She was living under the Japanese colonization before Kim [Jong Il]. People who lived before that time knew that it was different. But they kept their silence, and by the time he came to us, we didn't even know that we were slaves to a dictator. And so when they ask why there's no revolution in North Korea, I ask, 'How do you fight when you don't know you're a slave?' . . . We can't take freedom for granted—it's a very fragile thing."

Yeonmi then shared something that truly shocked me: She's not scared of what's *coming* in America. She's afraid of what's *here*. She came to fight for her people in North Korea but now finds herself having to fight for freedom in America too—a fight for individual rights.

To fight for individual rights is to be, in essence, an individualist. It's to believe that each person is of more value than any single role or function in society—that each is a unique, living, breathing, thinking human being—and as long as one person's freedom doesn't directly infringe on someone else's, then you're good to go. In other words, lots of power given to individuals and less power for government, groups, or institutions.

By having an understanding grounded in the US Declaration of Independence—that life, liberty, and the pursuit of happiness are *birthrights* and that the government can't give it to you nor take it away—this right here, folks, is truly the only way to make progress on a national level and still be authentically inclusive. Because where a true democracy exists there will be individualism, and where individualism exists there will be a true democracy.

The term *individualism* itself was first coined by Alexis de Tocqueville's *Democracy in America*. Tocqueville, forever the invested far-off onlooker, understood American democracy—what he called "the equality of conditions"—not merely as a way to govern but as a way to live.[1] Individualism was a *lifestyle*, not rooted in selfishness but in self-reliance, empowering the individual to be dependent on no man nor entity other than himself.

But this also meant that there was a distinct kryptonite for the individual—a make-or-break thing that this young, budding democratic experiment hinged on: *other* individuals.

This is where it gets interesting. Tocqueville knew then that there was a danger in the shadows. He feared that democratic individualism would produce a "tyranny of the majority." In essence, he warned the majority could easily amass too much power and impose large, sweeping systems of control on local communities.[2] The result would be a society not comprised of independent people but instead reliant on large, centralized systems that they wouldn't be able to survive without. (Think: *What if Google deleted your Gmail account? What if Chase bank decided you couldn't bank with them anymore? What if Amazon removed your website?*)

A centrally ruled society risks devaluing individual freedoms.

Eventually this kind of democracy morphs into a creepy little monster. The monster has a name. A horrible name.

The collective.

The Collective Doesn't Exist

While dystopia may feel imminent, utopia, my friends, is fiction.

Currently, there are about 333 million people living in America—that's more than 130 times as many people who lived in America at the time the US Declaration of Independence was written—and here we are *still* trying to smooth out the political and philosophical wrinkles in this great ongoing experiment in democracy that Tocqueville warned us about.

It's never going to be perfect. Sure, it would certainly be a heck of a lot easier if America was made up of one monolithic, singularly thinking collective. I mean, we'd look like North Korea (again, very little social unrest going on there)! But instead it's made up of 333 million diverse *individuals*—all with different stories, ideas, dogmas, and backgrounds. America was an idea that everyone can come from every walk of life—whatever religion, region, nationality, sexuality, and skin color—and come together to make this nation better. Although we arrive at the proverbial American dinner table equal, our lives and beliefs will differ because *we the people* differ.

Or at least that's true to some extent. It seems that there are some things we can agree upon.

According to a study by the Cato Institute, nearly two thirds of Americans said the current political climate prevents them from "saying things they believe because others might find them offensive." The percentage of Americans who self-censor has risen several points since 2017, when 58 percent of Americans agreed with this sentiment.

These fears cross partisan lines. Majorities of Democrats (52 percent), Independents (59 percent), and Republicans (77 percent) all agree they have political opinions they are afraid to share.

The survey found that many Americans think someone's private political donations should affect their employment. Nearly a quarter (22 percent) of Americans would support firing a business executive who personally donated to Joe Biden's campaign. Even more—31 percent—would support firing a business executive who donated to Donald Trump's reelection campaign.[3]

This isn't all that surprising, is it? I mean, it's the twenty-first century. You're either woke or you're not, and to merely *think* out loud is to doom oneself to the collective's loud judgment and ultimately its cancel-culture gulag.

But these marginal differences in percentages highlight a much deeper point—one that I've been harping on for a while now on *The Rubin Report* and during my own political shift away from the Left: Although neither side is perfect, I find the Right to be *exponentially* more tolerant, way more respectful toward individuals, way more supportive of individual thought, way more interested in diversity, way more progressive, way more inclusive, and honestly, just a way more fun side. The Right is a toga party with a bunch of people drinking and smoking and sharing different and often competing ideas. The Left *thought* it was a party, when in reality it was just a mob of angry, sex-deprived people who kick people out of the "party" and who find themselves alone at the end of the night, calling the police because the party on the right is having too much fun—and then demanding we defund the police.

Put simply, the Left is for collectivism and judgment based on group identity; the Right is for individual thought, individual expression, and personal liberty. From an American perspective, people on the right believe in the US Constitution, meaning you believe that *all* people should have equal rights to pursue whatever it is they want, period. You don't give two shits about a person's gender, you don't care about a person's sexuality, or where someone came from, as long as that person is a legal, naturalized citizen. Individuals on the right believe that we should have equal laws for all people, and they believe in equality of *opportunity*, not equality of outcome. That's a foundational principle that in many ways sprung from the US Constitution. As mentioned, we didn't have it perfectly, but we eventually expanded those freedoms over time. We freed the slaves, and we gave women the right to vote and people the right to marry whomever they wanted.

Then there is the woke mob—small but mighty—creating a tyranny of the majority, not by numbers but by being the loudest, most active, and most oppressive. Always prowling. Always lurking. Always trying to suppress any form of individual thought: don't think for *yourself,* think as a *collective* (or don't think at all).

If we diminish the importance of individual thought and expression, we diminish free will. And if you take away free will, what are we? Not unique three-dimensional humans; just meaty blobs of genes.

In other words, if the individual mind isn't in control, it must be immutable characteristics like skin color or sexuality that are. So people start getting grouped collectively instead of being seen as unique. White people are evil. Black people are victims. If you're gay and you vote for this person, you're actually *not* gay. (Trust me, I've heard this one a shocking number of times.) Ultimately, collective grouping collapses into the idea that different groups need different rights, which is the opposite of what our founding fathers fought for, which is—wait for it—*actual equality.*

America was founded on the principle that the government's sole purpose is to protect the rights of the individual, not the collective. It was not to protect certain groups of Americans, whether identified by race, gender, age, or any other identifiers. And yet, here we are, being pressured to identify ourselves by our sexuality, gender, or the color of our skin. Pretty sure that is the reverse of what that Martin Luther King Jr. guy would have wanted, but who cares about him anymore, right?

Americans were even lumped into groups based on their response to the coronavirus itself. Thousands of people gathering to celebrate Biden's election: good! Thousands of people gathering for political rallies for Trump: bad! Protests for BLM: good! Protests for election fraud: bad!

No person or idea should be *expected* to join a side merely because of their skin color or sexual preferences. Do we expect one hemisphere of our thinking brain, with its right and left sides, to fully dominate and define who we are? Of course not. We've got to embrace our status as holistic individuals—as fully fleshed and (hopefully) fully formed autonomous people.

So, what happens if your thinking brain doesn't align with the white-hot collectivist-thinking of the day? The mob gets you canceled—and no one is safe. Take once-well-beloved author J.K. Rowling, for instance. She got canceled for tweeting, "Dress however you please. Call yourself whatever you like. Sleep with any consenting adult who'll have you. Live your best life in peace and security. But force women out of their jobs for stating that sex is real?" after

Maya Forstater, a British researcher, lost her job at a nonprofit think tank following a series of "transphobic" tweets. It wasn't long until a bunch of preteens in Sussex voted to drop Rowling's name along with Winston Churchill's (a guy who, you know, *literally* fought the Nazis) as house names. They haven't kicked Harry Potter out of Hogwarts yet, but I hear there is a petition.

Even adobo sauce got *cancelado*. (Thank you six months of Duolingo!)

Goya Foods, America's largest Hispanic-owned food company, which was founded by Spanish immigrants, made the cancel list in 2020. When CEO Bob Unanue said that America was "blessed" to have "a leader like President Trump who is a builder," in no time, #BoycottGoya started trending on Twitter. Of course, Representative Alexandria Ocasio-Cortez, queen of "the Squad," got in on the action, tweeting, "Oh look, it's the sound of me Googling 'how to make your own adobo.'"

Of course, everyone has every right to buy or not buy a product based on whatever reason he or she wants. You want to not buy beans cause you don't agree with the company's moral compass? That's great but, on the other hand, I can be gay and still love Chick-fil-A, which I do. That's just rational self-interest and laissez-faire capitalism doing what it does best.

But this isn't laissez-faire. This is just not fair. It's something more sinister than the free market or influencers influencing. Instead of varying individual thought being discussed, we're dissolving into a tyranny of the majority via the collectivist conformity that has emerged from the fear of not being deemed publicly woke.

The warning is clear: conform or be canceled.

The solution is even clearer: to loosely quote the Beastie Boys, "You gotta fight for your right to parrrr-take in freedom."

None of this is new. We're all tired of cancel culture. But remember, individuals exist—the collective does not. The cancel culture mob is a paper tiger. It gets its power from our acquiescence—from our fear and silence. The only way to beat it is to stand for what you believe in.

I consider myself a world-weary optimist. Eventually, the Left will purge all their freethinkers, and with that the Right will actually expand and create the widest, most inclusive tent in the history of politics.

Our current dystopian reality has made it necessary to embrace our God-given rights in a world where the old labels don't make much sense anymore. No, you don't need to be a card-carrying member of the Republican Party with a picture of Ronald Reagan in your kitchen. It simply means that you want to conserve some of the greatest and most timeless Enlightenment principles. It means that you believe that *everyone* is deserving of life, liberty, and the pursuit of happiness.

If you're feeling politically homeless, stop and answer the following questions. Do you believe people have the right to a fair trial if they're accused of wrongdoing? Do you believe people have the right to express their opinions in public? Do you believe that all Americans are equal under the law, no matter their race or religion? If you answered yes to any of these questions, congratulations and welcome—you have joined the side that has any chance of creating a decent future (and your gift basket is in the mail).

Don't Burn This Book was a call to free thought; this book is a call to action in a time when the stakes for keeping a principled society have never been higher. This book is not only a survival guide to our scary world but also a manual for saving the country. It is a call for freethinkers, left-wing refugees, and yes, conservatives to resist the liberal "woke" agenda and adopt a forward-looking mindset. Within this book you'll learn how to:

- Dismantle systems of structural stupidity: With the crumbling of all our institutions and the disintegration of tradition, comes the disappearance of common narratives we once unified around. Chapter two is about attempting to find a moral compass to steer by in the face of our culture of wokeism, which employs radical ideologies to destabilize society. If America is going to weather the current storm, we as individuals need to become the kind of people worthy of freedom and understand the forces that undermine it.

- Protect yourself against propaganda: The minute you minimize the screen time and consume media with caution you'll realize that there's a whole world out there for the picking! Instead of mindlessly consuming misinformation, fake news, agenda-touting entertainment, and just plain bad TV, chapter three alerts you to be aware of the content you consume and attempt to create new forms of content as a way to keep your brain and the world around you from rotting.

- Declare digital independence: Many years ago we all joined social media thinking it would be a place we could connect with the world around us, but for the most part it just made us angrier, more divisive, and less special. In chapter four, we'll take a look at the current landscape of Big Tech and discuss how to be technologically savvy and relevant yet still possessive of what's rightfully yours in order to be an active participant and not just a product.

- Embrace your inner black sheep: The past two years have taught us that those in power will never let a crisis go to waste. Chapter five will challenge you to decide what you will and will not do when the pressure is on and when the powers that be start flexing their authoritarian muscles.

- Prepare for the worst: The modern world is obsessed with self-care, but what we really need is self-reliance. When the shit hits the fan, can you take care of yourself? Can you change a tire? Can you successfully grow a garden? Can you make a roaring fire? Can you forage for food? We'll talk about basic survival in chapter six, sure, but also how to thrive in the midst of a dystopian reality. We'll take a look at the progress we've made as a society, which has been extraordinary but has also made us all wildly dependent.

- Destroy socialists, as they say, with facts and logic: People like to think money is the root of all evil, but the reality is it's our out-of-whack relationship with money that's evil. Chapter seven reviews how our welfare state keeps our most marginalized suppressed while individualist principles, like capitalism and the free market, empower individuals to be self-sufficient and pursue a more enriching life.

- Avoid what I like to call The Eighteenth-Century Lesbian Poetry Trap: Our lives, and more specifically our careers, have taken on a tired and antiquated pattern. People go to college, graduate with a useless degree, drown in debt, accept jobs that lock them into complacency for years, and then die. This is no way to live. Chapter eight will show you how to think about school and work differently—both as an employee and a business owner—and how to eradicate useless activity from your life so that you never waste your time (or anyone else's) again.

■   Become a hero, not a comrade: More than anything, communists hate true community. Conversely, America is nothing without it. Because if we aren't good spouses, good parents, good kids, good colleagues, good neighbors, how can we expect to have a good society? Chapter nine will outline the differences between the collective and the community and how you should opt for ways to strengthen your most meaningful relationships so you can live a life worthy of celebration.

By reintroducing free will, choice, diverse ideas, and philosophy into the debate with the understanding that *these* are truly the things that shape the world, we'll elevate the debate beyond screaming matches and name-calling into a vibrant new philosophy.

The Future Is Now

Look, I get it. If you're less inclined to have children, you're less inclined to care that much about the future.

Knowing that I'll one day have a child to raise changes everything. Although I've always cared about the future of this country, something is different now. It's personal. I have to ensure that my children and grandchildren inherit a better world than the one we're living in . . . or at least one that's not worse.

Every generation has something to fight for. Maybe twenty-first-century generations happen to find themselves at the beginning again—needing to fight for a system that is, indeed, *by* the people and *for* the people. But here's the thing: it's not just going to just magically become better. In fact, I don't believe anyone is going to do it for us. I believe we have to do it ourselves.

The collectivist Left wants to strip you of those intrinsic and personal choices. You should want to stay home. *In fact, you'll get paid for it! You can watch porn and play video games all day and, when doing so, are actually helping people!* But I believe that by making good decisions for ourselves, we can resist the insane world the woke elite have created. By being honest, working hard, cultivating good relationships, making beautiful things, contributing to the world, raising a healthy family, and so on, we can create a great society.

Oddly enough, I think most wokesters have good intentions. They honestly (albeit idiotically) think that they're doing what's best for people. It's not that Chinese takeout and Fortnite are intrinsically bad, it's just that most of us—and I really do mean most of us—want something *more*. Most of us want to openly and honestly discuss real issues to try and pave a path forward. Most of us want to thrive. (Actually, come to think of it, I've seen some of those videos of people playing Fortnite on YouTube and it does seem pretty horrible.)

We don't want to be numbed and silenced and kept in the dark. We don't want to be controlled by a small fraction of hysterical people amplified by algorithms and media. We don't want to live like hamsters in a cage, being fed once a week and occasionally being put into a plastic ball that will undoubtedly fall down the stairs. (Sorry, Chippy!) And yet, for so long we've allowed the system to control us with curated and filtered information, politicized rhetoric, and fear-inciting communication. Maybe the communication circus, the philosophical freak shows, political performances, and the cultural carnivals will wake us up to find our lives, our families, and our livelihoods on the line.

So will we sit back and let the worst take control? Or will we find free will where we once found fear? Will we find allies where we used to find enemies? Will we stand for principles even when it's not popular to do so? Will we fight for liberty—personal liberty, economic liberty, social liberty, and cognitive liberty? Will we fight for a thriving future?

We're at a pivotal moment. You know it. I know it. You know that I know it. I know that you know it. So what are we going to do about it?

Well, I've got a few ideas . . .

2

DISMANTLING SYSTEMS OF STRUCTURAL STUPIDITY

Every record has been destroyed or falsified, every book rewritten, every picture has been repainted, every statue and street building has been renamed, every date has been altered. And the process is continuing day by day and minute by minute. History has stopped. Nothing exists except an endless present in which the Party is always right.

George Orwell, *1984*

I Don't Give a Shit if You're Gay

It was December 21, 2019, eleven days after they formally announced Donald Trump's impeachment inquiry. I was in Florida to speak at the Turning Point Student Action Summit. The day before I arrived, there was a rumor going around that the president was going to speak at the event. Sure enough, after some speaker cancellations and a bunch of rescheduling, I ended up essentially opening for the President of the United States, and I gotta say, I was glad all those years as a stand-up comic had prepared me for that moment. And sure, while it was surreal, it was by far the *least* surreal part of that day.

After President Trump spoke, I went backstage with my husband, David, when Donald Trump Jr., who at this time had become a good buddy of mine, approached me and asked, "Hey, you guys want to join us for dinner tonight?"

His girlfriend, Kimberly Guilfoyle, chimed in: "We've got a table for four! Can you join us?"

"Oh great. Where?" David asked, thinking it would be some nice restaurant in West Palm Beach.

"Mar-a-Lago," Kimberly said.

David and I looked at each other, simultaneously thinking, *Thank God we brought suits.* That night, we were supposed to go to a black-tie event that Ben Shapiro was headlining, but instead, only a few hours later, we were en route to *the* Mar-a-Lago (sorry, Ben). As you'd expect, security was insane—after a long jaunt around a small island, they all but stripped us naked before throwing us into the back of a golf cart. We arrived at the front entrance and it felt like I was stepping into an even gaudier version of the Playboy mansion— covered in gold and doused in hairspray. It was Donald Trump in building form.

Someone showed us to the main dining area, where about fifty people were sitting for dinner. We recognized a few familiar faces and said hello to some of those we knew personally, including Candace Owens and her soon-to-be husband, George Farmer.

Then, surprisingly, we were whisked away to a smaller side room in which about twenty were seated. Here, we went through yet another layer of security. They told us to keep our phones in our pockets and that no pictures could be taken, and then showed us a table smack-dab in the middle of the room, where Don Jr., Kimberly, David, and I were all seated.

I looked to my right. One table over was President Trump, First Lady Melania, Rudy Giuliani, and two other people.

So when Junior asked, "Hey, you want to meet Dad?"

I sarcastically say, "Uh, I *guess* I'd be willing to meet the President of the United States . . ."

We stand up and take a couple steps over to the table.

"Dad, this is Dave Rubin . . ."

Trump looks up and says, "Hey, I think I recognize you."

"Oh, well," I say, "I go on Fox and *Tucker Carlson* quite a bit."

"Ah, that must be it," he says. Then he turns to my husband. "And you—who are you?"

"I'm his husband!" David said.

"Husband! You two are married?" He squints his eyes and smiles. That's great!" In pure Trump fashion, he slapped his hands on the table and stood up to shake our hands. "You guys are too good-looking; that's your problem." He smiles and looks us straight on: "Ya know, I don't give a shit that you're gay. And I don't think anybody else does either. And I don't think anybody has for thirty years."

Looking back, David and I realized that his forwardness was likely because he thought that *we* thought he was a homophobe. That's what gays have perpetually been told by the media. In a very Trump way, he didn't want to beat around the bush and instead wanted to make sure we knew he was, in fact, *not* a homophobe. Honestly, it was refreshing. We weren't being pandered to. It was just Donald being Donald.

The conservative movement has come a long way since the George Bush era of antigay initiatives and referendums, capitalizing on a massive evangelical voting bloc headed by former RNC Chair Ken Mehlman, who spearheaded those initiatives only to, of course, come out as gay years later. And lest we forget, Barack Obama was actively against gay marriage when he ran for president in 2008. (I'll bet ya a crisp five-dollar bill that the so-called tolerant progressives of 2040 will want to take down his presidential portraits someday too.) It's funny; if people stopped and thought about it for one moment, they'd realize Trump was the first openly *not* homophobic president. (Sorry, Barack, but you ran against gay marriage the first time around. By woke standards, you're a homophobe for life!)

In many ways, it was harder coming out as a Trump supporter than coming out as gay (and it was not easy to come out as gay). Nowadays, culture will treat you like a war hero for being gay and a turncoat for being pro-Trump. But it was that moment on December 21, 2019, that solidified it for me: Trump was the *ultimate* individualist. He is immensely and profoundly flawed, of course, but will we ever have someone working in the political system who is more human? Who is more authentic? Who is more uncensored, unrestricted, or honest-to-a-fault than Donald J. Trump? He was and always will be an over-the-top renegade. But what happens when a renegade fights the system? The system crushes them. It chokes out every ounce of character, goodness, decency, and humanity. He was no savior—just some cartoonish businessman who made some smart choices and unmasked and exposed the system to show it for what it is.

Think about it. Trump was the first president in modern history to *not* start a war (and in fact started peaceful dialogue with enemies like North Korea). He cut taxes, cut regulations, and created millions of new jobs, bringing unemployment down to 3.9 percent.[1] Trump targeted racism at colleges and universities by attacking Critical Race Theory. But, alas, the system doesn't care about peace, prosperity, or equality; the system only cares about control and politicians only care about politics. Imagine that.

The fact that he could get *anything* done while the media made it their sole mission to take him down is impressive in and of itself. But the guy managed to actually expose that bias too. Perhaps best of all, he shook up both political parties, descended into the swamp, and fought the bureaucratic creatures who dwelled there as hard as he could. But as he eventually found out, the swamp always finds a way to drown out any ounce of authenticity.

Love him or hate him, President Trump did what most weren't willing to do: see something broken and try to fix it. If we can humanize the guy who eats steak with ketchup, stares childishly into a solar eclipse, and caters McDonald's to the White House, then there has to be an inkling of admiration for somebody who gave up his cushy life—and donated his presidential salary to charity—to be willing to do what no one else would.

Trump didn't become the orange catalyst for good, or evil—depending which side you're on—overnight. He was *always* the guy who would do stuff when no one else would. In 1986, Trump was a rising real estate developer with an office that overlooked Central Park. There from his view was the famous New York City disaster called Wollman Rink. Since 1980, this historic ice skating rink had been shuttered and set to be restored at the cost of $4.7 million. By 1985, the construction project was $12 million over budget, and the rink was still a pile of rubble.

Enter Donald. He stepped in and offered to rebuild the rink in six months. The work was completed two months ahead of schedule and at a savings of $750,000.[2] Asked why he wanted to take on the project, Trump said it was the "last thing I wanted to do, actually." But he wanted to see the people have an ice rink.[3] Maybe he rebuilt it out of the goodness of his heart, maybe it was a cunning business plan, and maybe it doesn't matter. All that matters is he stepped up to the plate and successfully did the thing that no one else could.

If you can grant me a long enough leash to say that the guy is *not* Hitler, you can see that he got some good results. But calling President Trump "Hitler" is exactly what the progressive Left did, and once it did that, there was no amount of good deeds done that could have saved him. Once someone is labeled Hitler, it's very problematic to suddenly say, "Hey, wait, that Hitler guy isn't so bad!" So, instead, the progressive Left chose to double down. Again and again and again and again.

Ironically, Trump did something similar.

If you ever watched old videos of a young Donald Trump on shows like *The Phil Donahue Show* and *The Oprah Winfrey Show* (where Oprah, believe it or not, *kinda* said the racist Nazi should consider running for president in 1988), you'll notice a of couple things. First, you may notice that his message was almost exactly the same as it is today: a practical and populist message about the political elite screwing over the everyday American. Trump was grounded in those beliefs (which are not something most of his politician counterparts can share). Second, was his soft, thoughtful, deliberate, prudent delivery.

People don't develop deep-seated political beliefs overnight, and Trump is no exception. Something happened to young Donny when he went bankrupt in the early nineties. After years of being sneered down upon by other billionaires and the media, something clicked in his brain and turned him into a counterpuncher. He had to get even scrappier and started making his money in nontraditional ways. He became the underdog in virtually all circles. From real estate mogul to reality show celebrity, the new Donald became a brand largely by way of his punchier demeanor. But, ironically, in turn, he was taken less seriously, so the fire got stoked. It was a vicious circle. To prove himself, he doubled down on the harsh rhetoric and unstatesman-like behavior as the stakes got higher. His internal beliefs stayed the same, however; it was the rough and orange packaging that changed.

Of course, Trump made mistakes and didn't always surround himself with the best people; but the mainstream media doubled down on flimsy, unfounded beliefs and claims (and lies). I am not sure if it was a philosophy, an ideology, or a divine being that enabled Trump to set his sights on something more than what was right in front of him and to therefore not give a shit about what people were saying, but he had to have a belief in *something* bigger coupled with a reluctant acceptance of knowing he had to do something about it.

Beliefs are kind of like boats. If they're firm and built well, they can keep you afloat when the tides start rising and the waves get choppy. But if the boat is inflatable and the beliefs are just full of hot air—not based on any real knowledge of *why* you believe what you believe—the minute someone pokes any holes in them, you're in trouble. You'll start desperately clinging to something that will do nothing but drown you. And you can only tread water for so long before you sink.

The Progressive Postmodern Parasite

Christ Church Cathedral, St. Mary's Tower, the Exeter Chapel spire—Oxford University is the oldest and arguably the most beautiful and respected university in the world—and with each mast and spire, its skyline exhibits its millennium-long beliefs.

I had the privilege of speaking at Oxford University in the summer of 2018, and let me tell ya, it takes walking down those ancient streets in person to understand how long people have been fighting in service of good ideas. As you meander the cobblestone streets and look up at the towering architecture, you feel the university's overwhelming and weighty history.

For nine hundred years, thousands of students have participated in things like taking Mass and sitting for exams wearing fancy garb to uphold these beliefs. Through monarchies, tyrants, wars, Nazism, and communism, Oxford University maintained these traditions while still managing to conduct intense religious debates with academic rigor.

And yet, in these "unprecedented" times, Oxford University is crumbling. From students voting to ban conservative Christian groups (so much for intense religious debate) to equity and inclusion statements from the *Physics* department (so much for academic rigor), in recent years, a quiet, patient parasite crawled inside its walls and began to eat at the structure from within, resulting in hysterical politics crushing our youngest and most promising. What is this subtle and discreet parasite, you ask? The woke social justice movement. And it found a nice, warm host among the heart of academic institutions, telling us that the intellectual compass we've been operating with was faulty, providing us a shiny, new, constantly recalibrating one.

Of course, it's not just Oxford University. It's the entire education system. In fact, most of us can loosely remember the timeline of the rise of the social justice movement in direct correlation to the appearances of college campuses in the headlines. It seemed to coincide with conversations around sexual assault and #metoo—an admittedly complicated subject. But, instead of attempting to weigh the facts and give the accused fair hearings, college administrations ultimately considered it sexual assault on women anytime alcohol was involved (talk about feminism!). That moved on to conversations around race, such as when colleges like Evergreen State College in 2017 instituted a "Day of Absence" to ban white people from campus. Oberlin College in Ohio canceled classes in 2013 for the day when reports came in that the Ku Klux Klan had infiltrated the campus—turned out it was a girl doing the walk of shame with a blanket thrown over her head to hide her face. Next comes the conversation around gender, where Dr. Jordan Peterson, some little-known professor at the University of Toronto, stood up against a bill that passed in Ontario making it obligatory for professors in classrooms to use the chosen pronouns of the student. So if a student insisted on being called ze or X, he was legally obligated to use that pronoun in referring to them and could actually face fines and ultimately the possibility of jail if he failed to do so.

Okay, we see the catching of the parasite. We see the spreading of the parasite. But where did this parasite come from?

My friend James Lindsay, a lifelong liberal (in a good way!) and a *Rubin Report* guest, spends the better part of his life trying to answer this exact question. The book *Cynical Theories*, which he cowrote with self-proclaimed "liberal humanist" and British author Helen Pluckrose, seeks to explain the rising popularity of the social justice movement. I call it "wokeness," some call it cultural Marxism, but James and Helen use the term *postmodern Theory* (with a capital *T*).

James and Helen boil postmodern Theory down to two key principles. The first principle is intellectual: an intense skepticism about whether objective truth, or knowledge of that truth, is possible. The second is political: a belief that society is formed by systems of power and hierarchies that decide what can be known and in what way. When these principles are applied, consequences often occur: boundaries get blurred, specialized language becomes a tool, truth becomes subjective, and the individual disintegrates.

It didn't happen overnight. In fact, according to James and Helen, there are three phases of postmodernism. The first took place in the 1960s and '70s and was mostly academic, exploring concepts around the nature of knowledge, power, and language and focusing on the works of Jacques Derrida, Michel Foucault, and Jean-François Lyotard. In essence, phase one instructed, *Be skeptical and distrust everything.* Think: *Is two plus two really four . . . why not five?*

The second phase was in the late twentieth century and early twenty-first, when those ideas mutated, solidified, and were applied to political realms, including colonialism, race, and gender. Think: *Perhaps math is just a product of racist imperialism?*

The third phase, which they say began around 2010, is called "reified postmodernism," which spotlights real-world activism and beyond. Think: *We must stop teaching math to children because it's racist!*

One of the most pervasive postmodern Theories is Critical Race

Theory, which, as Manhattan Institute Senior Fellow Chris Rufo defines it, is "identity-based Marxism." CRT is currently infiltrating virtually every school and government agency in the country, but a recent incident in Seattle struck me as particularly disturbing. In 2019, Seattle Public Schools released a new curriculum aiming to "re-humanize" mathematics. It suggests that Western mathematics had been used to "disenfranchise people and communities of color" by posing as "the only legitimate expression of mathematical identity and intelligence." The curriculum's new learning objectives ultimately ask, "Who gets to say if an answer is right?"[4] (And that's not exaggeration on my part, it's directly quoted from the proposed curriculum.)

Yikes. Orwell wrote in *1984*, "Freedom is the freedom to say that two plus two make four. If that is granted, all else follows." Who would have thought he'd be so spot on?

Postmodernism began innocently enough—it was rooted in philosophy and acted as playful cynic and questioner. Nothing wrong with that. I do the same thing and encourage everyone else to as well. But instead of just letting the creature live, we fed it and fed it and fed it. And we didn't just feed it. We inflated that creature, pumping it with steroids until what was once a cute, mischievous little Gizmo became a horde of flesh-eating Gremlins.

Real-world activism is where the whole postmodern thing went off the rails. In modern parasitic terms, it's like when the coronavirus went from "a bat in China," to one infected person in China, to the whole damn world . . . but then the world got crazy and destroyed itself beyond what the virus could ever have done in the first place. (As of this writing, it seems like everything reported to us was a lie, and the new coronavirus that emerged to cause COVID-19, named SARS-CoV-2, may actually be a leaked bioweapon from a lab in Wuhan, China, that was conducting gain-of-function research.)

Another shocking example can be found in the summer of 2020 at the Smithsonian National Museum of African American History and Culture. As part of a virtual exhibit called "Talking About Race," a description of "Whiteness" and its traits were presented. It contained a chart that described white culture as including traits like rational thinking, hard work, being polite, and the scientific method.[5] (Ironically, a mode of thinking that is literally the strongest tool to remove your own biases, racial biases included. Imagine that.) The goal was to reveal guidelines for talking about race, but then those guidelines, in turn, became totally racist! Call me a bigot, but I don't think hard work, politeness, and critical thinking are for white people only . . . insane, I know.

Athlete Michael Jordan worked harder than anyone. He practiced more than anyone else in basketball history. Good god, the guy won an NBA finals game when he had the flu. Is the Smithsonian suggesting that Jordan was just emulating Larry Bird's work ethic?

Right off the bat, a sane person who sees people as unique individuals would have said, *Um no. Hard work and rational thinking belong to everyone, not just white people.*

The postmodernist, on the other hand, regards things like "hard work," "reason," and "science" as oppressive and a flexing of power when utilized, essentially implying, *You cannot access these Western ideas because you're black.* By their logic, according to them, if you're black and you're an engineer, you're a phony or you're not really black.

It's frustrating, yes, but it's not all doom and gloom, folks. The beauty of the parasite is that it ultimately doesn't stand a chance against the truth—and the people who believe in the truth. The obsessive activist woke weirdos spare nothing, and anything that merely falls in line eventually crumbles. After significant pushback on social media, the Smithsonian eventually took the graphic down and apologized. But the fact that anyone working in a government-funded museum thought this was a good idea in the first place proves that the damage has been done and the host has been infected.

It's kind of like when Joe Biden said, "Poor kids are just as bright as white kids" and "If you have a problem figuring out whether you're for me or Trump, then you ain't black." The progressive wokesters' obsession with race makes them say absolutely crazy things that end up being genuinely racist and seriously problematic. (To be fair, I don't think Biden is racist, I just think he has been experiencing severe cognitive decline. Hey, nobody's perfect.)

For most logical, non-woke, liberal-in-the-true-sense-of-the-word people, knowledge and objective truths that stand the test of time and hold fast from culture to culture are considered attainable. For woke postmodernist progressives, there is no such thing as truth—only social constructs to be dismantled. James and Helen put it like this:

> Postmodern Theory and liberalism do not merely exist in tension: they are almost directly at odds with one another. Liberalism sees knowledge as something we can learn about reality, more or less objectively; Theory sees knowledge as completely created by humans—stories we tell ourselves, largely in the unwitting service of maintaining our own social standing, privilege, and power. . . . Liberalism values the individual and

universal human values; Theory rejects both in favor of group identity. . . . Liberalism encourages disagreement and debate as means to getting at the truth; Theory rejects these as ways of reinforcing dominant discourses that suppress certain perspectives [and] promotes the idea that truth is a "language game." . . . Liberalism accepts criticism, even of itself, and is therefore self-correcting; Theory cannot be criticized.[6]

This language game births new terms that get applied at a huge scale at the exact same time they are being defined and culturally deemed "true."

Take the new term *antiracist*. It's cleverness and trendiness embodies the language game being played. No longer can people be *not* racist. Now, they must be *anti*-racist. What is anti-racism you ask? Ibram X. Kendi, author of *How to Be an Antiracist*, tells us:

> The opposite of racist isn't "not racist." It is "anti-racist." What's the difference? One endorses either the idea of a racial hierarchy as a racist, or racial equality as an anti-racist. One either believes problems are rooted in groups of people, as a racist, or locates the roots of problems in power and policies, as an anti-racist. One either allows racial inequities to persevere, as a racist, or confronts racial inequities, as an anti-racist. There is no in-between safe space of "not racist."[7]

If this feels like a foreign language, it's because it kind of is. With such new, unfamiliar terminology, it takes time to translate and define. Ben Shapiro did a bit of interpreting in his article "The Problem of 'Anti-racism'" and perfectly summarizes the anti-racism movement:

"Racism is no longer defined as someone believing someone is inferior because of their race. Now racism is the belief that *any* group differences can be attributed to *anything other than racism*. So, any system that ends with different outcomes must be racist."[8] In Kendi's words, "Racism itself is institutional, structural and systemic."

No longer is racism defined as a personal belief that does not correspond to the reality of equality. For the anti-racist, there is no such thing as the reality of equality of individuals. There is no reality at all but only social structures that can either be built or dismantled. To be anti-racist is to actively tear down institutions and systems via that real-world activism, "reified" phase of postmodernism. This means that everything must fall under the microscope and ultimately be destroyed. Actions like working hard, being polite, and employing the scientific method, sure, but also things like *real* equality and America's culture of inalienable rights. Suddenly, concepts like "equality" are too idealistic, which is why it's being swapped out for a new and improved term, *equity*: meaning that instead of making sure everyone has equal opportunities, we will ensure that everyone's lives suck equally. For progressives, it's not about reducing racism; it's about destroying institutions that all Americans rely on. You have to give them credit: tearing some people down to make everyone the same is a lot easier than building some people up.

Ironically, as an intersectionalist, Kendi believes that we should take all the supposed oppressed groups—black people, trans people, gay people, and fat people—and combine them into one stronger thing to fight against the system. In his words, "To truly be feminist is to be antiracist. To be antiracist (and feminist) is to level the different race genders [. . . and . . .] we cannot be antiracist if we are homophobic or transphobic."[9]

As we know, this just ends up turning into an oppression olympics where nobody wins.

The irony? On January 25, 2021, Kendi made some less-than-woke remarks at an online seminar held on Zoom titled, "How to Be an Antiracist School."

> "Last week my daughter came home and said she wanted to be a boy, which was horrifying for my wife to hear—for myself to hear. And of course, you know, we're like, 'Okay, what affirmative messages about girlhood can we be teaching her to protect her from whatever she's hearing in our home, or even outside of our home, that would make her want to be a boy.'"

Wait a minute! That doesn't sound very intersectionalist or antiracist to me, you transphobe! Is he admitting that his daughter's gender is not simply a social construct, but reality?

In all seriousness, that very moment should have destroyed the entire intersectionalist woke movement—the whole house of cards should have come crumbling down. Here is Kendi, the main thought leader who wrote the wokester's bible, accidentally admitting it was all bullshit! Why was he so "horrified" that his child might be trans? This should be considered ideal according to his own magical dictionary. But it's inevitable—the woke mob cannot keep up with its own wokeness.

Wokeness arose in opposition to the claim that truth is objective. The idea of universal truth, whether scientific, religious, or philosophical, is distasteful to the woke. Just like a parasite, postmodernism can't *be* a host—it cannot have any new ideas or solutions—it merely infects and garners its power from deconstructing already existing ones, subtly and completely.

This is the elegance of the parasite. It's intelligent and discrete, and recalibrates what you know to be true. It infects and deconstructs until there is nothing left.

It reminds me of one of my favorite sci-fi movies, *Alien*. You know, the one directed by Ridley Scott with Sigourney Weaver where the alien bursts out of that guy's chest? The crew of the starship *Nostromo* is awakened from their cryosleep capsules halfway through their journey through deep space to investigate a distress call from an alien vessel. The plot thickens when the crew encounters a nest of eggs inside the alien ship—one of which affixes itself to Executive Officer Kane.

What follows is a spoiler alert, although I am not so sure if spoiler alerts count after forty years. If you haven't seen it, besides the fact that you should be wildly ashamed of yourself, I recommend that you skip ahead a bit.

When Officer Ripley (played by Sigourney) discovers Ash (the science officer) has been secretly ordered to bring the alien back despite it risking all of their lives, she confronts Ash. After some violent head-to-head and a surprise reveal that Ash is not even a human but an android, Ash expresses admiration for the creature:

> **Ash:** You still don't understand what you're dealing with, do you? The perfect organism. Its structural perfection is matched only by its hostility.
>
> **Navigator Lambert:** You admire it.
>
> **Ash:** I admire its purity. A survivor . . . unclouded by conscience, remorse, or delusions of morality.

I am not going to lie to you. I, in some strange way, admire this thing. I admire its purity. I admire its delusions of morality. Its effectiveness is freaking *impressive*. You have to give the devil his due.

I hate to say it, but we can't save the already infected institutions. I never wanted them to fail; my preference would have been that they stood up for liberalism when they had the chance. But they have become figurative Officer Kanes; sad and unfortunate victims to their own beliefs. If you believe in nothing other than what you're told based on a political or cultural agenda, it's not only impossible to survive—it's dangerous to the others on the starship. Remember, there are about 333 million people living in America. If each individual compass is recalibrated according to fleeting opinions and feelings, there is no way we'll ever know where true north is. We'll never know what's right or wrong, fact or fiction, reality or fake news.

The good news is the progressive postmodernist Left has encountered a few problems. How could it hold the crumbling cultural structure together while simultaneously trying to destroy it? And if it only knows how to destroy, how can it save itself from that destruction?

For a while, its members thought tolerance could be their antidote to prevent their own infection. Yet, who are the most intolerant people in society right now? It's the people who are telling you constantly how tolerant they are all while calling you a racist, bigot, homophobe. Yes, you!

This is another example of the "language game." Tolerance *sounds* great. It's gentle, kind, and accepting. But tolerance allows everything to exist except that which it considers intolerant. This is where the progressive postmodernist Left begins to infect itself. Its own philosophy renders it incapable of policing its own people and finds itself forced to turn to—and this is where it gets hilarious—the *government* to make laws.

Wait, I thought racism was *systemic*? I thought the government was a giant patriarchy? The very institution and structure that the Left deems most oppressive and intolerant ironically becomes the structure it is forced to strengthen to promote its agenda. (It's an idea so idiotic that you'd need the next *Alien* movie to be directed by Michael Bay instead of Ridley Scott.)

Ask yourself: What more can the government do to save us? Is there even one law I would want passed right now? Now, you might answer, "I want free health care for everyone!" Okay, well first of all, that's not a law. That's a massive federal governmental program, and do you know of any giant government programs that work? If so, what are they?

The assumption that an institution is meant to solve anything is the reason nothing ever gets solved at all. It's like what ol' Ronald Reagan said: "The nine most terrifying words in the English language are: I'm from the government and I'm here to help."[10]

Which is why the problems of today can only be solved by a shift in *belief.*

So, if man and man-made institutions can't save us, what can?

The God-Shaped Hole

We're all born into this world with a deep hole. No, not that hole. No, not that one either! Come on people, this is a family-friendly book ... kinda. I'm talking about the elusive, tenuous God-shaped hole. Most ignore it, many drown it with drugs and alcohol and video games, some fill it with knowledge, and the rest of the mere mortals fill it with an archaic belief of something known as "God."

Some of us (read: me) have done all of the above.

Despite growing up around religious stories, from Hebrew school to Seder, to Shabbat, to Yom Kippur, I was never able to fully understand the need for faith. I was always one who favored knowledge over belief, but Jordan Peterson helped me bridge that gap (as I mentioned in my last book). It was during Passover 2021, however, that my beliefs fully took root.

The Passover story goes that the Pharaoh started to worry that the Jews would outnumber his own people in Egypt. His solution? Kill all the firstborns and enslave all the rest. Then came Baby Moses, who was put in a basket, floated down the Nile River, and ironically was saved and adopted by Pharaoh's daughter. When Moses got older, he was commanded by God to lead the charge of freeing the Israelites. Cue: *Let my people go!* The Pharaoh said no, so God stepped in and began the Ten Plagues—everything from blood to boils, frogs to locusts. Before the final plague, Moses tells the Pharaoh that all the firstborns in the land of Egypt would die. The Jews are told to mark their doors with the blood of a lamb so that God would "pass over" them. Finally, the Pharaoh gives in and lets the Israelites go, but as they escape, the Egyptian army chases after them. When they reach the Red Sea, Moses is commanded by God to raise his staff. The sea parts and the Jews cross. On the other side he's commanded to raise his staff again, and the sea returns to normal, drowning the Pharaoh's army and finally freeing the Israelites. (Pretty impressive I can remember all that from the Charlton Heston movie. . . . There's also that scene where he saves a bunch of talking apes.)

After being locked up and watching most of our civil liberties be stripped away during the year leading up to Passover 2021, the idea of freedom hit differently this time. The story of Passover is one of individual freedom—freedom from all the powers of the world, freedom *from* worshipping false gods, and freedom *for* the worship of a true God.

The Pharaoh was the leader of Egypt—not just politically but socially. He wanted to be worshipped and he wanted to be worshipped above everything, God included. Thousands of years later, our leaders aren't much different. Instead of worshipping Pharaoh it's worship of Big Government. What was once faith in God is now faith in "experts." Instead of God's justice it's social justice.

I remember the distinct feeling of waking up politically, but during those two Seders of Passover 2021, I had a deeper spiritual awakening—one that was a long time coming. I finally felt a spiritual hunger (or maybe that was because I didn't put enough horseradish on the gefilte fish).

For a long time I thought knowledge and enlightenment was enough. I hate to say it, but it's that very love of knowledge and enlightenment that led Nietzsche to scrawl his famous words, "God is dead." He didn't write that in celebration either. It was a warning—a warning to the Germans cautioning that once you've killed God, man will replace that with something else.

That's just what we as a society have done via the progressive woke parasite. The irony? The woke progressives have become the very things they hated—institutionalized, dogmatic, bible-thumping, religious, intolerant proselytizers. But to say it is a religion gives progressivism too much credit. Instead of institutionalizing a church, it institutionalized the universities. Churches are the houses of belief, but universities are the houses of education where their job is to create, legitimize, and pass on knowledge. Religions are forced to treat their beliefs as beliefs. Social justice has arranged things in such a way that it can treat its belief as undeniable fact.[11] Which is why progressivism ain't no religion; it's a cult. Instead of the Ten Commandments, it's political correctness. Instead of any meaningful spiritual awakening, it's a performative *woke*ning.

Turn on the news. Open your social media. Within moments you're being preached to about equity, diversity, anti-racism, and inclusion. Even in entertainment, whether a basketball game or reality show, it's hard to get through anything without getting some fire and brimstone sermon on sexism, homophobia, transphobia, or racism. What's worse is in modern America, people believe the CNN reporter, the sports announcer, or their college professor more than God, Jefferson, or Einstein.

Trust me. Politics as a religion makes societies really awful. Politics should never be the only way someone views the world. The people that endlessly think about politics are the ones that are constantly hysterical, constantly want to control you, and constantly want to tell you how to live. And why wouldn't they? Wokeness is their path to salvation.

In the Judeo-Christian tradition, original sin is considered something you're born with. There's nothing you can do about it except try to be a better person and find redemption. By the grace of God, you confess and try to cleanse yourself of it. For the woke believers, privilege is that original sin—and if you're an able-bodied, straight, cis, white man, you're unredeemable. Go to hell, Chad.

Just like a cult, the progressive collective provides an alternative community for us. Anyone who's watched a good cult documentary can spot the signs. Move over, Branch Davidians, Scientology, and

Nxivm, there's a new sheriff in town. *You don't need your God-given family or your religious community, you need the collective, your chosen family.*

The classical liberalism I have championed for years does not emphasize this need for God enough. Yes, tolerance and freedom are necessary for a functioning society, but the eternal truths told for thousands of years through historical and biblical stories are the rudders that keep us moving forward during this storm. This isn't to say that individuals can't be godless and still be good—but this is about how humanity can flourish over time and withstand the human forces that want to enslave and impoverish us. This is about how to enforce our own values over someone else's. The only antidote for that is a truth outside of *us*. To be a good person means to seek truth, and to best avoid slippery solipsistic subjectivism, sometimes you have to seek eternal truths outside of yourself. Remember, anything made by man can be destroyed by man, and so the ideals of freedom and equality have to come from somewhere beyond just the human mind—somewhere unchanging and everlasting. With all the insanity wreaked by the day-to-day news—when we can't believe anything we hear anymore and when information is wholly corrupted—is it really *so* hard to believe in these ancient, powerful stories?

I get it. It's a mess out there. But that's what faith is all about. In April 2021, I had a conversation about Passover on *The Rubin Report* with Rabbi David Wolpe and Bishop Robert Barron right at the tail end of Passover and right before the Easter weekend. Rabbi Wolpe shared a small piece of the story that I somehow always missed in Hebrew school: "The most common thing in the Torah that God says is 'Al Tirah.' In English it's 'Do not be afraid.' That is the single most indispensable quality needed to lead a good life: courage. Without courage you're a slave. When the Israelites left Egypt, they stood at the sea—it wasn't until one man (Nahshon) jumped into the sea that the sea parted. Because God wanted them to take a risk.... Life is in part about jumping into the sea."

All Hands on Deck

While the conservative movement certainly needs to define itself by traditional American values, I am in no way advocating a return to old-fashioned Republican prudishness. If this movement is going to have any legs, it needs to be a home to everyone who opposes the woke regime. Regardless of your views on foreign policy, taxation, climate change, or, yes, even abortion. If you oppose the woke regime, you are welcome here.

The conservative movement has reached an interesting moment, arriving at a rare opportunity to welcome millions of people who now consider themselves politically homeless. It's no longer Right versus Left. It's not red versus blue. It's woke versus everyone else.

You can have the conservatives that are more traditional and God-fearing (who want the government out of their lives so that they can continue to maintain these beliefs) and then you can have the conservatives that err on the secular, libertarian side (who want the government out because mo' government means mo' problems). Despite my deepening belief, I still identify more so with the latter. While the two camps may differ on existential issues, there is an opportunity to work together to protect the American experiment, save our Enlightenment ideals, and gather around a central, objective belief of individual rights.

So, how do we take the more traditional, religious conservatives and blend them with the refugees of the Left?

If we really want to create the most amount of freedom for the most people—if we want to create a space where a majority of people can think for themselves—we have to gather as an anti-woke alliance even if we don't agree on every issue.

Of course, it will never be perfect. I mean, again, we're not trying to create a religion here! Ironically, most people in favor of authoritarianism think that if you can make their views the dominant views of society, that you'll have a "more perfect" society on the other side. Leftism is the idea that imperfect humans can create a perfect system. It's the belief that if everyone could behave within that perfect man-made system under government power—that if everyone could be woke—life would be a utopia. But this belief can only lead to dystopia.

Which is why they got it right in the Preamble of our Constitution (emphasis added): "We the People of the United States, in Order to form a *more perfect Union . . .*"

They didn't say *perfect*. They knew that wasn't possible. So they shot for "a more perfect" union.

It will get messy, and there will be disagreements. Do you think that when our founding fathers wrote the US Constitution it was peaches and cream and no one disagreed with anything? Of course not—but they worked together to rethink a better way to live and create, not a perfect, but a *more* perfect union. No doubt, many duels and drunken bar fights resulted from the long days nailing down this fancy document, but in the end, they all signed it anyway.

Imperfection is where a healthy tension can foster. We will agree on the big stuff enough so that we can always be debating and sussing out the details. And we don't need to even figure out the big religious questions, specifically because the founders gave us the tools (i.e., separation of church and state plus religious liberties) to best ensure that humanity's unanswerable questions didn't get in the way of the quest for a more perfect union.

If you believe in individual rights—if you really believe all this we're saying about the individual and freedom—then you're going to have to be okay with having some folks on your team who are different than you and at the same time, try to keep the wheels on this whole America thing so as to gently roll forward.

Now, I am in no way saying that conservatives shouldn't hold fast to their values and even try and holistically spread those values. In fact, I think now is the time more than ever to do so. Laws, regulations, systems, and structures won't save us. Family, hard work, personal responsibility, and hope will. And not to sound like a right-wing maniac but you can even keep that patriotism stuff—a pride in our flag and our country.

But while you hold on to what you believe, also be open to other ideas and remember, certitude is poisonous. When you're certain of everything, you can never learn anything. Like my great mentor Larry King said after years of interviewing those across the religious, ideological, and political spectrum: "The only thing I know is I don't know." Take in ideas. Stay curious. Think critically.

It's up to you to figure out what you believe. Just believe in something... and good God almighty, let it be more than politics.

3

PROPAGANDA PROTECTION

Brawndo has electrolytes: they're what plants
crave.

Idiocracy, 2006

Off the Grid

Every August I take a break from the digital world. For thirty days, I put away the phone, shut down all social media, and lock up the laptop. No tweets, no texts, no calls, no news, no nothing. Instead, I hike, read, go to the beach, and go fishing. Ya know, human stuff.

But even after five years of doing this, the first couple days of the shutdown is always tough. Habitually, I'd reflexively reach for my pocket. But by day four or five, the anxiety quells and instead—and I kid you not—actual *music* starts to play in my brain. Seriously. My brain starts to teem with melodies I had long forgotten. I feel actual physiological changes going on in my brain. I'm calm yet stimulated. At peace and yet stirred. Rooted in reality and yet more open to pondering deeper, more ethereal questions. In fact, it was while on one of these hiatuses I realized that maybe I wasn't an atheist anymore.

For a few of our "off the grid" Augusts, David and I would go to Bora Bora in the South Pacific. We would stay in one of those huts that sits on stilts right over the water, and it feels as if you've reached the end of the world. The turquoise ocean goes on for miles, the clear blue open skies stretch for eternity, the bright foliage, and the crisp air—it's about the most beautiful thing you can imagine. Each day, I'd go to the beach with nothing to do except be. Naturally, that would lead to some people watching. Every time, without fail, the majority of people would be sitting in lounge chairs scrolling through their phones, taking a video of the waves (again), sitting at dinner texting while their partners checked their emails. Like reverse evolution, everyone's backs were hunched and heads were down. The minute you step away from it all you see how truly inhuman and abnormal it is.

More quickly than I'd like to admit, however, I'm back to doing the same shortly after I get back on the grid. But, man, those thirty days are about the most humanizing and restorative thing you can imagine. What's ironic is this was how we all lived just a few decades ago.

Going offline for even a few hours, let alone a few weeks, feels like a superhuman feat these days. In 2019 (pre-quarantine, mind you), American adults spent about three hours and thirty minutes a day on their phones.[1] In 2021? An estimated four. So, if you do the math of even just three hours and thirty minutes a day, that means in just thirty years we'd spend 1,825 days—that's a little more than four freakin' years—*on our phones*. This doesn't even include the other times we're staring at screens watching television or getting work done on our computers.

We can barely remember pre-2007 when there was no such thing as iPhones or "streaming services." Do we even remember when we used to have to wait a week to watch the next episode? When people would *do* things as they waited for the once-a-week, thirty-minute 8:00 p.m. sitcom time slot? Nowadays, instead of making a nice meal in anticipation, we indulge in feverish benders of binge-watching or accessing the twenty-four-hour news cycle 24/7 with constant notifications. Whatever, there's no need to cook anyways—we've got Postmates.

I'm not going to sit here and tell you that these things are all evil, and I'm actually not even demonizing our little black mirrors. I even watched the show *Black Mirror* on my little black mirror. Plus I have the most incredible job (if I can even call it a job) on planet Earth because of it. But the ability to live life not constantly connected is going to be more crucial the more that our carbon lives merge with our digital ones.

The biological repercussions are simple enough: eyestrain, neck pain, headaches, bad posture, weakening of brain muscles. It ain't looking good. But what about the way we *think*? What about the way we understand the world and those around us?

The danger isn't just how *much* we consume, although your bed sores, unwashed hair, and glassy eyes might say otherwise. It's the subtle messaging, the slight physiological tweaks, the brain numbing, the inclination to believe things that deep, deep down you know can't be true.

Or worse, the fact that you literally don't know what reality looks like anymore.

The War on Reality

Typically, when I come back from my monthlong respite, there is some big news.

Someone will say, "Dave, you will not believe what you missed!"

Oh, I promise you, I can.

Man, what a surprise, AOC said that? Congress still hasn't passed that bill? A bomb exploded in the Middle East? A song called "WAP" hit number one? (Okay, that last one I actually couldn't believe—and I'm still confused what the bucket was for.)

In reality, very little news makes a huge impact on your immediate, day-to-day life. Maybe a storm or occasional tsunami can rearrange your travel plans, but most of the time a headline doesn't immediately affect anything other than your mentality, or in the most unfortunate cases, is reporting something bad that has already affected you.

A century ago, political commentator and writer of *Public Opinion* Walter Lippmann argued that mass media is less about delivering truth and more about acting as the main connection between what went on in the world and what went on in our brains. The first chapter, titled, "The World Outside and the Pictures in Our Heads," opens like this:

> There is an island in the ocean where in 1914 a few Englishmen, Frenchmen, and Germans lived. No cable reaches that island, and the British mail steamer comes but once in sixty days. In September it had not yet come, and the islanders were still talking about the latest newspaper which told about the ap-

proaching trial of Madame Caillaux for the shooting of Gaston Calmette. It was, therefore, with more than usual eagerness that the whole colony assembled at the quay on a day in mid-September to hear from the captain what the verdict had been. They learned that for over six weeks now those of them who were English and those of them who were French had been fighting on behalf of the sanctity of treaties against those of them who were Germans. For six strange weeks they had acted as if they were friends, when in fact they were enemies.[2]

On the island, the tone changed quickly once they got the news of WWI. The moment its inhabitants were told to hate one another, hate one another they did. Today, what happens when we are notified for each and every worldwide update, minute-by-minute? Our pocket constantly buzzes with information (both true and false) that determines how we should feel, think, and behave. Like Pavlov's dogs with iPhones, we're trained to salivate over who to love (don't forget to subscribe to my YouTube channel!), who to shame, who to hate, and who to cancel. Virtue signaling perpetuates it beyond the news cycle so that no matter the source—informed or not, trusted friend or unknown influencer—we react and act based on how we're told to.

Immediately following the story of the island, Lippmann mentions the famous cave from Plato's *Republic* that describes people as cave dwellers, tied to their chairs, spending their lives watching shadows on a wall and thinking it's reality. When one of the guys breaks free, he leaves the cave and sees reality for what it is. Eventually, he returns to the cave to tell his still-confined friends the truth, but they won't believe him.

Hmm, sounds a little familiar does it? Some things don't change.

You might have heard me say that we are currently in the middle of "the war on reality." Depending on what you read or watch on TV, you may actually live in a completely different universe than someone who doesn't consume the same media. Mainstream outlets like CNN and MSNBC are not in the business of news-making. They're in the business of world-shaping. It's no wonder everyone is so mad about politics all the time. How can you see eye to eye with someone when you live in separate galaxies?

In fact, the main point of Lippmann's *Public Opinion* was to illustrate the problem facing democracy "because the pictures inside people's heads do not automatically correspond with the world outside" and to propose a solution based on a "representation of the unseen facts." It was Lippmann who first identified the tendency of journalists to generalize based on ideas and not facts. He argued that people, including journalists, are more likely to believe "the pictures in their heads" than to come to judgment by critical thinking.

He goes on to warn that democracy itself would be at risk of endangerment "if the propagandists and censors can put a painted screen where there should be a window to the world."[3] The critique on democracy, similar to what Tocqueville warned us about when he discussed the "tyranny of the majority," was that general public opinion would merely be those pictures in our heads being collectively acted upon rather than actually based on reality by individual thinkers.

It's like we're locked in a cave of media misrepresentation and we all take the shadowed pictures as an *accurate* reflection of what's actually happening in the world.

News Flash: It's not. The media doesn't *reflect* reality; it filters and shapes it. (And sometimes makes it up altogether!)

Most of us know that by now. Trust in traditional media is at an all-time low and has been in steady decline for quite some time. The majority of people (56 percent to be exact) believe that journalists and reporters are purposely trying to mislead, and 58 percent think news organizations are more interested in ideology than facts.[4]

As I said before, I'm a world-weary optimist. I don't think the news and Big Media were always that bad. I believe that there was a time when journalists tried their best to share information and cover worldwide events with integrity and courage in an attempt to make sense of a complicated world.

But throughout the last few years, we have watched journalists in the mainstream media morph into dishonest content curators to construct preapproved narratives—or in layman's terms: partisan assholes who have worn out their outrage-o-meters.

When people think of fake news, they usually think of it two ways: (1) a completely fabricated or factually false story, or (2) when, for the intent of getting more clicks, the title of an article has almost nothing to do with its substance. In 2016, I had Eric Weinstein on *The Rubin Report* when he broke fake news into four simple categories. (I also go in-depth into this in my last book, *Don't Burn This Book*, but will summarize them again here cause I always wanted to quote myself quoting someone else in my own book.):

1. Narrative-driven fake news is when the outcome is predicted and editors work toward that outcome.
2. Algorithmic fake news describes how Big Tech and social media manipulate our news based on who and what we click and follow.

3. Institutional fake news is where a highly respected organization releases a study and passes it off as objective fact because . . . "experts."
4. Blatant falsehoods are just what they sound like: outright lies.

The type of fake news that I think is most interesting (and most dangerous), however, is the kind that we see constantly on air—and by that I mean *don't* see. This is the type of fake news presented to us when the media refuses to discuss stories that are counter to the narrative they want to tell. Throwing care and integrity to the wind, they're willing to destroy people's lives and careers for one thing and save people for the same, carefully selecting the winners and losers of the stories they're telling.

For example, the sexual-assault allegation made by Tara Reade, a former Joe Biden staffer. In the midst of the 2020 presidential election cycle, a clip was circulating widely on YouTube and Twitter from over twenty-five years ago when Tara Reade's mother called into *Larry King Live* on CNN and talked about her daughter, who had been having issues with a sitting senator.

The story had been catching fire online. It seemed like a desperate mother dealing with her daughter's pain, trying to reach out for advice. Yet the media had completely ignored it for the most part. Why? Joe was their pick for winner, so they covered for ol' Joe with a Mafia-style protection racket. And yet, not two years earlier the mainstream media had totally annihilated conservative Supreme Court nominee Brett Kavanaugh during his Senate confirmation proceedings for similar sexual assault allegations made by Christine Blasey Ford. Why? The Mafia protects its own and Brett was from the rival gang. Even worse than the NY versus NJ Mafia-like rivalry in *The Sopranos* is the Democrats (plus media) versus Republicans.

A more recent example is the Hunter Biden *n*-word fiasco. In June 2021, a series of lewd, foul text messages between Biden and George Mesires were released in which Biden playfully called Mesires, his white attorney, the *n*-word several times. Only "fringe" publications like the *New York Post* and *National Review* covered the story, giving Democrats license to dismiss the incident out of hand. I'm not here to police the guy's private life or language, but do you think the media might've covered the president's son's use of the *n*-word if the son had been Don Jr.?

When they outwardly lie about a story, that's one thing, but when they hide a story from viewers, it becomes the viewer's responsibility to figure out if there is a story at all. It makes ya wonder—with so much focus on one thing, what else are they missing? What else are they ignoring? Is it because it's not important, or is it so important they have to snub it?

But look, it's not just ignoring negative news around the Left—it's ignoring positive news about the Right. The Media Research Center tracks evening newscasts on ABC, CBS, and NBC, and noticed a variety of positive stories about conservatives that had been skipped time and time again.[5]

Here's another example, and this one is a doozy. On March 15, 2021, *The Washington Post* made a massive retraction to a January report about a phone call between President Donald Trump and a Georgia elections investigator placed on December 23, 2020, including several quotes attributed to Trump that were given by an "anonymous source." The article originally reported that Trump implored the investigator to "find the fraud in the state" and that she would be a "national hero" if she did. A recording of that phone call, however, revealed otherwise. His statements were taken completely out of context. As you can imagine, the correction was not circulated nearly as far and wide as the original story. What's worse is that other major news outlets ran with the original story, going so far as to confirm it. Among them? CNN, Vox Media, and the NBC, ABC, and USA Today networks. Guess which entity followed up with front-page corrections to the widely spread article? Zilch. Nada. Nil.

Not only did these media outlets make up what became a massive scandal, but this story was also weaponized as part of Trump's second impeachment (remember that two-day sham?). What's interesting is not just mainstream media's dishonesty and the fact that no one ever gets fired for faux journalism—it's the way that a lie can start and then work its way through all of the mainstream. Then it becomes up to us—you, me, everybody—to pilfer some truth out of the endless river of nonsense that they make us swim through.

What's so dangerous about mainstream media is that if you don't fully accept the narrative hook, line, and sinker, you're called a conspiracy theorist. Oddly enough, this is why I have sympathy for *actual* conspiracy theorists! After years of being gaslighted by the news, they were pushed into a corner of paranoia, only exacerbated by being called crazy lunatics. For years everyone was told to question Trump's legitimacy as president, but the minute the mainstream got what it wanted, to question then became a double standard. To question the November 2020 presidential general election even ever so slightly puts you on a far-right list. When a conservative says something, it's "violence," but when a wokester says the same, it's "courage."

It's time for the media to take some responsibility for pushing certain people into conspiratorial corners.

It reminds me of a famous quote generally attributed to Soviet dissident Aleksandr Solzhenitsyn: we know they are lying, they know they are lying, they know we know they are lying, and yet they continue to lie.[6] I probably should just get that tattooed on my face at this point . . . would certainly make my job easier.

In case I need to state the obvious: not every person who works in media is an evil, Oz-like villain. Most of these folks are just people who wanted to tell stories in some way, shape, or form. In fact, they want to do good, and that's what makes them dangerous—the compulsion to do what they think is good or right at the expense of the American public's right to know the truth. These people often graduate with a degree in journalism or political science and get jobs, those jobs have bosses, and those bosses have a boss and that boss is the American public. Except there's one caveat here: the American public has a publicist and that publicist is the collective mob.

If you don't believe me, ask MSNBC commentator Chris Hayes. Although I disagree with him on nearly everything under the sun and think he looks like a muppet pretending to be a newsman with those thick-rimmed glasses, I'll give credit where credit is due. When the Larry King video of Tara Reade's mom was circulating around, Chris Hayes was willing to—and, guys, you will not believe this—actually *cover* the story. A journalist doing journalism is as rare as Chelsea Handler saying something funny. This made Hayes one of the few prime-time hosts to address the allegations on his show. His point was correct: if we're going to take allegations seriously, we have to take *all* allegations seriously. The Me Too movement was purportedly about listening to *all* women . . . but I guess that really meant only the women who support the stories the mainstream media is telling.

And as it goes in the Twittersphere, no good deed goes unpunished or slips under the radar. In moments, #firechrishayes was trending on Twitter.

Which connects it back to Lippmann's and Tocqueville's point: Does fault lie with the press, or with that portion of the public—that is, the collective, the mob, that small but loud and crazy minority—who demands to be told what it wants to hear? Is the line between opinion and fact so blurred that we can't tell one from the other anymore? This is why, at the end of the day, my main concern is not that the government is coming for my freedom of speech. My primary worry is that we are doing it to ourselves. We are the ones actively silencing ourselves. We are the ones who unfurl the mob on one another, and no matter what you may think, the more you feed that mob, the more likely it is that it'll eventually come for you too. (Yes, even you Chris Hayes.)

We've got to be active and engaged participants in the democratic nature of news. The media wants lots of eyeballs on its content, including yours, so if you aren't speaking out against the fake news and the mob mentality, reporters will naturally assume that what they are doing is working. Don't let people who are simply louder than you, speak *for* you.

And as we watch mainstream media collapse, it's even more likely that we're all going to withdraw into our own little ideological echo chambers. The temptation is warranted, but we can't just consume only the things we agree with and listen to only those things we want to hear. Fact can never be about preference. While it's a nearly impossible task, try and take in information from across the ideological spectrum so you can see things in a wider context and dilute the risk of forming single-minded inclinations. (For example, watch the "Direct Message" segments of *The Rubin Report* live on YouTube every weekday at 11:00 a.m. Pacific Standard Time, and watch *Rubin Report* interviews with clips dropping throughout the week!)

We've got to see the whole story and prioritize facts over bias—because *that,* my friends, is how we end this war on reality.

Streaming the Mainstream

I had to promise my editor that I would limit my *Star Wars* references to just one to land this book. So here's my one plug. Promise.

Anyone who knows me at all knows that I am a sucker for sci-fi—*Contact, The Matrix, Alien, Total Recall,* I love 'em all. But *Star Wars?* Oh boy, that one's special. I can't even remember the last Halloween I didn't go as a character from *Star Wars.* I was Kylo Ren in 2019, Obi-Wan in 2018, and Anakin before that.

But, along with the rest of our institutions, the parasite saves nothing.

I was not a fan of the last *Star Wars* trilogy. It was scattered at best. There was seemingly no attempt at trying to create a cohesive story, so each director sort of had his own crack at it. J. J. Abrams wrote something for *The Force Awakens,* then Rian Johnson basically completely aborted that story in *The Last Jedi* (and it suffered terribly for it), and then Abrams came back to try and fix the whole thing in *The Rise of Skywalker,* but it was already too late.

Then there's *The Mandalorian.* It appeared on Disney Plus and brought the franchise back to life a bit (although full disclosure, while I liked it, I didn't think it was all *that* great). One of the lead characters, Cara Dune, played by Gina Carano, was a fan favorite, a former rebel-alliance shock trooper. She wasn't a princess, she wasn't a damsel in distress, she was just a kick-ass soldier and the audience loved her for it.

Gina is a talented actress, a fitness model, and a prize-winning mixed martial artist. She also happens to be a conservative (or at the very least non-woke). She was pretty vocal in 2020, outwardly questioning COVID-19 mask mandates, commenting on election security, and standing up against the mob when it attacked people with different views. Naturally, that culminated in #FireGinaCarano trending on Twitter. Following mob orders, Disney ended up canning her, and she found out that she'd lost her job not through her boss but via social media. Clearly, Disney needs a better HR team.

The reality is that the *Star Wars* franchise had been dead for years. Don't take my word for it, just ask any true fan. But I had been hesitant to put it to rest. I was hoping for a resurrection. I wanted it to be saved. My childhood was at stake! Plus, what was I going to do with all those Halloween costumes?!

But this was the nail in the coffin. RIP mainstream Hollywood. What was once a dream factory is now a recycling center. If you take a look at the top ten movies of 2019, you'll notice none are very original. Among *Star Wars: The Rise of Skywalker,* we had *Avenger's Endgame, The Lion King, Toy Story 4, Frozen II, Captain Marvel, Spider-Man: Far from Home, Aladdin, Joker, It Chapter Two.* All in all, it's a blasé mix of remakes, adaptations, sequels, or films based on characters of prior works.

The main reason, of course, is money—valuing revenue and power over originality and quality. Blockbuster movies cost anywhere from $100 million to $350 million to produce, so they need a guaranteed buy-in from the general public to make a return on that hefty investment. And that much money means there is a whole bureaucratic totem pole that is giving approval before the thing ever hits the silver screen.

This is why mainstream opinion is probably either wrong or late. By the time the Oscars decides something is cool or *The New York Times* writes about a new trend or a movement, it's probably already changed into something else. Those who have authority—including moral authority—are usually late to catch on. Even the publishing industry is not immune to today's fickleness. I'm writing this in late 2020/early 2021, for example, and this won't hit shelves until 2022 . . . assuming an asteroid doesn't kill us all by then.

The system is slow, but wokeness is fast. Wokeness isn't based on any real objective truth, so it's more like a soup of the day than an entrée mainstay. Plus, considering a movie often takes two years to get through announcement, preproduction, shooting, and post-production, what's woke today will be in a coma tomorrow.

All this is to say, Hollywood is lame. But then again, Hollywood feels like it's dead and gone already. Does anyone *really* watch the Oscars with bated breath, admiring the bravery, artistry, and courage of those making more money in a twenty-minute cameo than some will make in their lifetime? (Wait, what about all that essential workers talk? Why aren't you Hollywood folks taking pay cuts to pay our grocery store cashiers?!) Wokeness has ruined the very industry it emanated from to the point it can't even get a comedian to host the thing anymore because of fear of being canceled.

With Hollywood crumbling, a stronger woke machine was needed—something faster, fresher, more addictive. Something with a wider distribution and a shorter bureaucratic totem pole.

Perhaps a streaming service could make the mainstream even bigger, murkier, and with more infested waters?

Enter Netflix.

Since 2013, Netflix has produced its own shows, releasing programs that are more and more politicized. Without the restrictions from the Federal Communications Commission, and liberated from the pressures of advertisers due to its subscription-based model, Netflix gained full control over the content it created and distributed. And because all income is generated by the viewers, this model also gives the company an extra layer of freedom to pursue said political agenda. (Are we sensing a pattern here or is it just me?)

Thus, Netflix has released a deluge of original political documentaries and docuseries. Most of which—and this should come as a surprise to literally *no one*—are from progressive points of views. From *Get Me Roger Stone*, which criticized one of Donald Trump's top and most controversial advisers, to *Knock Down the House*, which casts a loving glow on progressive Democrats Cori Bush, Amy Vilela, Paula Jean Swearengin, and (naturally) AOC around their 2018 primary campaigns, they've left no political stone unturned. I mean, can you even imagine Netflix producing a show about up-and-coming Republican politicians that didn't focus on them being racist, homophobic bigots?

But it's not the blatantly political content that is the problem. At least you know what you're walking into with those. The more nefarious issue lies in the seemingly innocent: entertainment guised as propaganda packaged and promoted in such a way that you consume it ad nauseam.

Surprise, surprise, the term *binge-watching* rose right along with the rise in Netflix's popularity. This rapid consumption of streamed entertainment is now a part of our culture's ethos. In fact, a whopping 61 percent of users regularly watch between two and six episodes of a show in one sitting. Half the shows we binge-watch receive a glowing endorsement of "uh, it was okay." Twelve hours of your precious life for *okay*?

Turns out, the popularity of binge-watching wasn't a happy accident as a result of good content. It was very intentional. Netflix actively promoted binge-watching because its investors have been told it is essential to their existence. Back in 2011, Netflix CEO Reed Hastings was asked about the company's motivation for making entire seasons available at one time. His response? "Netflix's brand for TV shows is really about binge viewing," he said. "It is to accommodate, to just get hooked, and watch episode after episode. It's addictive, it's exciting, it's different."[7]

Hey, I had a drug dealer tell me that once!

During a conference call in October 2014, Hastings called consumers' desire to binge-watch a "universal value."[8]

Ah, yes, those coveted universal values like freedom, equality, and gorging ourselves on bad TV. Let us not forget the classic humanist writer Michel de Montaigne, who said, *A wise man consumeth* Stranger Things *in one sitting until his brain goes numb.*

On an earnings call, Hastings also told investors, "We get so much data about how people watch, how fast they watch, that it really propels our programming."[9]

Guys, we've got to start reading the fine print. We missed the part that our $8.99 a month subscription also cost us our souls!

Although you may not be binging political documentaries, those fun sitcoms, quirky rom-coms, and compelling dramas are embedded with the perfect amount of politicization that, even if you do spot it, is just subtle enough for you not to turn off. A nuisance, maybe, but enough to quit the series? No way. So streaming services like Netflix learn what amount of propaganda is just enough to keep you watching and continue their delicate slant leftward.

A quick look behind the blue, velvet curtain and we see why.

In the 2020 election, tech executives were among the top political donors. Who signed the fattest check? None other than Netflix CEO Reed Hastings, who donated more than $5 million—the largest chunk going to the Senate Majority PAC, a group backing Democratic candidates in the closest races, like in Maine, Texas, and Iowa.[10]

It's not just the CEO. According to opensecrets.org, in 2020, Netflix employees have sent 98 percent of their political contributions to Democrats, resulting in millions of dollars flowing to Democrat candidates and party committees.[11]

That money—coming directly from the pockets of subscribers—keeps the cogs of the machine nice and greasy. In March 2018, Netflix added Susan Rice, former national security advisor to the Obama administration, to its board of directors. I'm still trying to figure out why a TV app would need a national security advisor on staff—although I am sure our screens will have lasers pointed at us to make sure we laugh at the appropriate moments soon enough. And you'll be absolutely shocked to find out that only two months later, Netflix signed a $143 million deal for original programming with the Obamas' newly founded production company, Higher Ground. Surely Barack's plan is to give us nonpoliticized, family-friendly entertainment! I mean, why else would he accept that paltry $143 million?

Naturally, Netflix's longtime, unabashed agenda has worn on conservatives. YouGov, a brand-perception market-research agency, indicated that Netflix's positive-impression rating among Republicans in the US has drifted down 16 percent from the beginning of 2018 through May 31, according to BrandIndex data from YouGov. At the same time, Netflix's approval rating with Democrats has risen 15 percent in tandem. Wow, can hardly believe it.

Like most leftist institutions, it'll no doubt eventually destroy itself. I truly believe that over time Netflix will purge the true artists who got into the business to make movies and not propaganda, and those artists will be forced to go elsewhere. In fact, only days after her Disney dismissal, Gina Carano landed her next film gig with not another Hollywood behemoth but with Ben Shapiro's *The Daily Wire*. And not just as an actress either. This time she's going to develop and produce as well. I never sensed that Ben would be in an action movie, but he *is* a fast little guy.

It reminds me of the conversation I had back in 2017 with actor, producer, and director Mark Duplass on *The Rubin Report*. As someone at the center of Hollywood with individualistic beliefs, he found the best way to remain creative while filmmaking is to take Hollywood out of it. Smart man. So the minute he made it big in Hollywood, he leaned back into independently creating film and television in a way that he could not only retain control creatively but also create the kind of environment in which he could support up-and-coming actors and creatives. But as it turns out, Duplass's business spirit is directly tied to his not-often-discussed beliefs:

> I always joke that I really am as liberal as they come if you look at me on paper. Except, if you look at me from a business perspective, I am at the very least a fiscal conservative, but probably more libertarian than anything else. If you look at Hollywood as government, I'm like, "Get away. I don't want you

in my face. Let me do my thing. I know what I am doing, I'll handle it myself." I look at a Hollywood production and I see waste everywhere. You are spending one day's catering for a Marvel movie what I spend for a whole movie. It drives me insane.

So I guess the conservative idea of wanting to keep what you earned based on what you built has some legs here. . . .

Of course, the mob leaves no thinking man unscathed. A year later, Mark tweeted: "Fellow Liberals: If you are interested at all in 'crossing the aisle' you should consider following @benshapiro. I don't agree with him on much but he's a genuine person who once helped me for no other reason than to be nice. He doesn't bend the truth. His intentions are good."

Not surprisingly, in seconds, he got mobbed, deleted the tweet, and issued an apology (which pretty much inferred to the mob that Ben was a hateful, homophobic racist).

Ironically, my friend Ben Shapiro (who isn't the devil, though he may eventually play one in one of his own TV movies) was right when he said in his book *Primetime Propaganda*, "Remember that the people making TV don't merely want to entertain you; they want to influence you. They want you to think like they think. And unless you're aware of what they're trying to do, chances are you will."[12]

Don't Deteriorate, Create

Friends, there is a world out there. It's called the real one. The best way to win the war on reality—and the best way to prevent your brain from turning into mush—is to take your eyes off the screen, look at the world right in front of you, and be a participant rather than just a spectator.

This was how I created *The Rubin Report*. When I viewed the world around me, I genuinely saw no other option. Like Mark, after treading water in the mainstream and seeing not much more than uninspiring bullshit, I wanted to create an alternative and own it myself. I didn't want my political and philosophical evolution to be disingenuous, so I figured the only way to keep it pure was to do it myself. When I created it, it wasn't to document my journey from progressive to conservative. That was a by-product of being more than a bystander. Instead, I created *The Rubin Report* to give myself the space to be open to ideas and create that same space for others as well.

That space happened to be in my garage. One day, a camera replaced the lawnmower, studio lighting replaced tools, and a red chair replaced a car. It wasn't your typical studio but, hell, it looked better than most. (To quote Fox's Tucker Carlson when he walked into my home studio: "Holy fucking shit—you did it right!")

In that garage, I simply talked to people I wanted to talk to about things the mainstream wasn't talking about. At the time, I considered myself a lefty, and so what was on my mind was why liberals weren't acting liberal anymore. To explore that, I chatted with some liberal refugees—people like Sam Harris, Maajid Nawaz, Christina Sommers, Ayaan Hirsi Ali, and Douglas Murray, and then later Ben Shapiro, Thomas Sowell, and Jordan Peterson. Having genuine, open, and honest conversations with people thinking similar, albeit unpopular, thoughts helped me feel a little less crazy—a little less alone.

Thus, the "Intellectual Dark Web" was born in my 24 x 22-foot garage.

My point? Consume with caution. Be aware of different kinds of fake news, notice hidden agendas in blockbuster entertainment, and minimize distractions so that instead of being passively influenced you can be actively independent. Stop relying on the very things you're denouncing. Stop feeding the cesspool of bad and false content by absorbing it till you barf. Stop complaining about it. Get off your couch-potato ass and actually do something.

The best way to combat a rotting brain is to exercise it and strengthen it like a muscle. If you hate modern-day journalism because it doesn't do a good job of telling the truth, do your own research and write quality content. If you dislike most of the blockbusters because the stories are tired and the motives are greedy, make a movie. If you are disgusted with Netflix for touting an agenda, create your own platform and make your own art. If you hate the academic institution as it stands and want a return to enlightenment over politics, create your own university or refuse to support nor enable the idea that people must go to college at all. Don't continually be dependent on structures that do not support your values or what is objectively true. Those who are awake as opposed to woke have got to start building their own institutions, whether it's businesses, universities, publications, entertainment, or tech platforms.

But your actions don't have to lead to an enterprise or empire. They can be as simple as recognizing that you spent your entire weekend watching Netflix and eating junk food, giving yourself a slap on the wrist, and learning something new instead—even if it's not terribly useful. Sharpen your skill set, learn how to cook or speak a new language, learn to code, work toward running a marathon, go fishing—literally just *do* something. I promise, you have more free time than you think and your life will look a lot better for it.

The upside of 24/7 online access is that it means we have access to the greatest minds at all time. One of the reasons our university system is quickly collapsing is that, frankly, people are getting smarter. The year 2020 has taught us that instead of paying thirty grand a year to go to school on Zoom, you can watch YouTube lectures for free. (So, if you're gonna binge-watch maybe try a Jordan Peterson or Thomas Sowell lecture).

On a physiological level, if constantly being tethered to screens rots your brain, learning new things helps repair it. Learning new things increases the density of your myelin—the stuff in your brain that helps improve performance on basically everything—and stimulates neurons. This means the more you learn the *better* you learn. As a bonus, it can even help you stave off dementia, something you definitely don't want . . . especially if you're the current president of the United States.

If the conservatives really want to make America great again, they should start by thinking about what it was that made America great in the past—and more important, they should think deeply about what will make America great in the future. The answer to said greatness comes with human ingenuity, creativity, entrepreneurship, lifelong learning, and culture-making. When it comes to determining the success of a society, it's culture, not politics, that matters most.

If you want to save the world—if you want to achieve something *truly* meaningful—be creative. Be an entrepreneur. Begin a business. Make a film. Use your powers of free thought to figure out how to help others in a way that brings them a new and better product or service. Simply start by telling the story you would want to hear, and not with a political revolution or institutional reform. (I mean, have progressives like Bernie Sanders, Ilhan Omar, and AOC ever actually accomplished anything other than taking people's money?)

At the end of the day, the future American doesn't need approval from an institution or industry. The future American doesn't need a popular ideology to abide by. Instead, when culture-making, these future citizens will be honest, vulnerable, curious, authentic, and informed. It won't be about approaching the world with an ideological mind. Instead, it will be about thinking for oneself and being willing to make art that conflicts with one's designated "worldview," rather than to focus primarily on trying to get Oscar buzz, producer attention, or climb the mainstream ladder.

Ask yourself, What am I good at? What do I *want* to be good at? How can I be a contributing member of not just society but culture? How can I participate instead of just absorb? How can I thrive instead of let hours just slip away, enabling my brain to totally decompose into a pile of mush?

Dear future American, *create*. Don't make propaganda, make content that stimulates the heart, not just the brain. Don't join the creators of fake news. Don't embed secret messages to change the hearts and minds of people. Just be willing to see reality for what it is and make good things for the sake of making good things.

In a media landscape run by only a select few, who is going to choose truth and virtuosity over money and agenda?

In a world of shitty sequels, who is going to create the next *Star Wars*?

(Seriously, I need to know.)

4

THE DECLARATION OF DIGITAL INDEPENDENCE

> Do not let your fire go out, spark by
> irreplaceable spark in the hopeless swamps of
> the not-quite, the not-yet, and the not-at-all. Do
> not let the hero in your soul perish in lonely
> frustration for the life you deserved and have
> never been able to reach. The world you desire
> can be won. It exists . . . it is real . . . it is
> possible . . . it's yours.
>
> Ayn Rand, *Atlas Shrugged*

Patrons, Patreon, and Patrón

January 15, 2019, was the night I got wasted on a livestream downing shots of Patrón.

It was also the time I accidentally disclosed my private, personal email address to the general public.

But, most important, it was the night I deleted my Patreon account.

Patreon is a crowdfunding platform that enables personalities to get their audience's support in the form of pledges. At the time, we were making about $30,000 a month from about eighteen hundred patrons, and 70 percent of my company's revenue was sourced from the platform. When I decided to jump ship, my financial advisor thought I was bonkers, because any remotely sane businessperson would never voluntarily give up such a substantial percentage of their earnings. But I didn't care—enough was enough.

Before I digress, let's set the scene a bit and rewind all the way back to AD 2017.

The internet was abuzz with the news of Patreon deplatforming Lauren Southern, a reporter and commentator for Rebel News Network and well-known conservative provocateur (and former *Rubin Report* guest). According to Patreon's Trust + Safety team, Southern supported actions by Defend Europe, which chartered a vessel off the coast of Italy to track and stop what it claimed was conspiring between NGOs and human traffickers. On July 20, 2017, without notice, Patreon banned Southern, which naturally sparked a huge backlash from her supporters. When probed as to why Patreon staff had decided to ban her from the platform, Patreon cited concerns about Southern "raising funds in order to take part in activities that are likely to cause loss of life."[1]

Amid the firestorm, I reached out to Jack Conte, CEO and founder of Patreon, to see if he would be interested in coming on *The Rubin Report* to discuss some of the complexities surrounding the ban. I had zero expectations that he would say yes as Silicon Valley CEOs are notoriously impossible to reach. Needless to say, I was absolutely shocked when he responded with a quick and enthusiastic yes. I was even more surprised when he agreed to do it live.

Among the things we discussed in our live interview was the deletion of Lauren Southern's account, free speech, media censorship, and Patreon's corporate policies. Jack explicitly stated that Patreon's Terms of Use applies *only to content that is on the Patreon site*. He explained the company's *content* policy (he used that word a lot . . . like *a lot*, a lot) and overall evaluation method—something known as "manifest observable behavior." A phrase I had never heard before. According to Jack, "The purpose of using manifest observable behavior is to remove personal values and beliefs when the team is reviewing content. It's a review method that's based entirely on facts."[2] He also admitted that Patreon's lack of giving Southern fair notice or explanation was shitty.

Okay, great. I accepted his rationale and life moved on.

But a little over a year later, in December of 2018, Carl Benjamin, known better as Sargon of Akkad on YouTube, woke up to find that his Patreon account had been deleted without explanation and notice. This hit a little closer to home for me personally, as Carl was one of the first people to help me wake up from my progressive slumber. Sure, he is a bit of a self-proclaimed troll, reveling in poking fun at social justice warriors and making inflammatory digs. But because he publicly promoted Brexit and consistently criticizes modern-day feminism, radical Islam, and identity politics, he's automatically and unfairly put in the far-right bucket. He sent Patreon an email asking exactly why it had deleted his account, and hours later he received an answer saying that his account had been deleted due to a violation of its Terms of Use.

Unsure of the violation, he followed up asking for specifics.

A day later Patreon responded, "The creator in question used racial and homophobic slurs as insults in a conversation shared online."[3] As part of the explanation for why it banned Benjamin, Patreon published a transcript of a YouTube video.

A couple things were evident right off the bat. First was the fact that this had happened *outside* the Patreon platform, which, according to what Jack Conte told me *to my face on my show*, was not a violation of the community guidelines. In fact, it didn't even occur on Carl Benjamin's personal YouTube account. It was said in a conversation on another user's YouTube. This would be like citing a private conversation that you overheard at a restaurant and then getting that person fired from his or her job because of it. Second, it involved something that pretty much always gets missed these days: sarcasm. Sargon's use of the *n*-word wasn't to make fun of black people, but rather to mock the alt-right—the very people that use these terms in a pejorative fashion.

It was clear that no consistent standards were being followed. At any moment a Patreon member could wake up to find his or her account closed because of words said or actions done outside of the platform's own ecosystem. Just because it was, according to Patreon, unacceptable "manifest observable behavior."

The irony? Patreon staff failed to realize that the acronym for their method of "manifest observable behavior" is MOB. And that's exactly what it was. There was no real "evaluation method." If there were, Jack and his team would have quickly realized that Carl Benjamin was indeed *not* a racist and was, in fact, making fun of racists. It wasn't about any violation of community guidelines. Patreon staff just didn't like what this guy had to say in general.

So I called Jordan Peterson (as one does when the heavy hands of censorship begin pressing down). We had a few days off from being on tour and a break was long overdue—yet, suddenly it didn't feel like much of a break at all. After a long discussion, we realized it was time to leave Patreon. It would be foolish to continually become financially dependent and structurally reliant on a platform that could kick us off at any time for no authentic reason. But it was also more than practical—it was philosophical and ethical to stand up for the very principles that we were talking about on the tour. If we weren't going to do something about it, who would? Remember, this isn't just censorship (although that would certainly be enough); this was people getting the boot and losing their livelihoods.

Jordan and I announced our exodus: January 15, 2019. He canceled his account the classy way—quietly from a hotel in Sweden. I decided to get drunk on Patrón tequila while live on air from my studio in L.A., stumble my way through the Patreon deactivation process, and inadvertently share my private email address. I tip my hat to all you clever trolls who signed me up to an endless amount of porn sites and progressive politician mailing lists.

But all the while, it had me thinking, *Maybe it's time to practice what I preach and put my capitalist, individualist ideologies to the test. Again.*

For years I watched how censorship had infiltrated the modern media landscape. That's why I decided to build *The Rubin Report*. What didn't become crystal clear until later is that censorship hadn't been restricted to the realms of traditional media and government— it had been outsourced.

So, I started small and mostly out of necessity. I called my brother-in-law, who was a tech guy, and asked if he could build a simple subscription page on my website so that people could make monthly donations. It was a huge risk. I didn't know if it would work or if people would be willing to jump from Patreon to my personal website. Patreon made up 70 percent of our total income, which not only paid for me and David, who was the executive producer of the show, but it also paid all my other employees' salaries, health insurance, and overhead. Suddenly, it could be gone in the blink of an eye (or more like a Patrón-induced blackout).

But it did work. Our revenue was up 30 percent in only a few days. One thing that's great about the majority of humanity is that people typically like supporting others for being brave and doing the right thing.

So our income was no longer reliant on Patreon, hallelujah, but my videos and audio were still dependent on other platforms like YouTube. After Jordan Peterson and I announced our exodus from Patreon, step two toward digital independence was having my own technology to share audio and video and still retain ownership of it. I also wanted a chronological content feed to function as a way to share that content and allow for people to engage with one another. I'm not gonna lie—by completion it was looking pretty damn sleek.

I was proud, and I was satisfied . . . but not *totally* satisfied.

It was time to build something that could work for everyone so that other creators could own their digital home and have control of their online life.

Thus, my company Locals was born.

Before Locals, everything kind of worked in a top-down way. Big Tech companies told everyone what to do and how to behave, all the while we had no recourse as users or creators. For years, I gave YouTube a professionally executed show, with over a million audience members, that made *them* money, yet had zero contact for help when we hit a glitch. Think about it: Who do you call when your email gets hacked on Gmail? 1-800-Google? There are terms of service and user agreements that are designed to be so long and jargoned that they're never upheld evenly and are accepted without normal, everyday people having actually read the fine print. You need a lawyer on retainer reserved exclusively for user agreements. Plus, there's this constant underlying feeling that Big Tech companies are hiding something— now more than ever as they harvest our private data to sell to god knows who and continue to deplatform, censor, and suspend creators left and right.

Look. It's not that I hate Big Tech. On the contrary, I would love to work with 'em if only 1-800-Google would just answer their phones! It's that as our lives have become increasingly digital, we've lost control. This is why the goal of Locals is a classically individualistic one: to give every person—no matter what side of the ideological spectrum they fall on—a chance to completely own their digital lives. This is why it's *not* a digital platform: it's a set of tools to build a digital home.

I wanted a place where each creator could determine their own rules of conduct for their community and monetary threshold for access. My rules for my own digital home are easy. Essentially, don't do anything deemed illegal by a US court of law, no porn, and don't be a relentlessly trolling freak. Now, before you tell me I am censoring trolls, let me beat you to the punch. I absolutely believe in free speech, but this is exactly why I've approached the Local communities as a digital home and *not* a giant platform. Giant platforms have become the primary way we communicate—so when they silence people or ban people, you can definitely argue that it's an infringement on our ability to communicate in the digital public square. But in the case with Locals, it's *your* home and I'm pretty sure you don't invite people who call you an asshole into your home. But guess what? They can say whatever they want outside of your home. So, we decided that the best way to minimize trolls is by asking them to put some actual skin in the game. For example, my current subscription cost for community buy-in is a mere $5 minimum. (Some people even pay more just because they like me. Shout-out to you guys: I like you too.)

The beautiful thing about having a subscription-based platform is that it can be ad-free, data-protected, and you eliminate 99 percent of all the evil that's online. The reason there are a billion burner accounts on social platforms is there's no barrier to entry—people can have several accounts with dumb little avatar pictures and say whatever the hell they want with no accountability. It's funny the amount of times I watch very bright people—well-known authors, lecturers, and thinkers—hop on Twitter and argue with pink foxes and street fighter anime characters. So, for just a small barrier to entry we can mature the internet. We can keep most of the trolls out and keep the conversation elevated, sane, and hopefully constructive and stimulating. And hey, if they want to troll your Locals account, at least you're getting paid!

Part of the problem with other large platforms is that everything online is "free." But trust me, there's no such thing as a free lunch. The price you pay is in fact quite expensive.

Think about it. We already learned how politically biased and data-motivated Netflix is. It costs $8.99 plus our souls—so, how much more do we think we are giving up when a platform is free?

The reality? If you aren't paying for the product, then you *are* the product.

With any free online service—Twitter, YouTube, Facebook, Snapchat, Instagram, Google, TikTok, you name it—your data is the product that is being harvested, targeted, retargeted, and sold. We would all expect to pay for a car if we wanted one, just as we would expect to pay for any other good or service. Yet for some reason the majority of people believe that these online services are "free." They are not. It's just like the history of mainstream media. Although TV networks didn't collect personal data anywhere near the way that Big Tech does today, they carefully studied their audience demographics and pitched that information to advertisers to create the most targeted ads possible. But, as we know, what started as curating purchasing choices evolved into cultural collapse.

Just like the business of mainstream entertainment has little to do with entertaining these days, social media has little to do with people being social. I mean, come on. We joined these social media platforms thinking it would connect us with our long-lost friends and long-distanced family—and it did, at the beginning—but over time this virtual connection eventually revealed that you disagreed with most of the people you loved. Disagreement should be well and good, but with the cover of anonymity and the comfort of sitting at our computers, typing things that you would *never* say to your aunt Verna's face, it devolved into the darkest side of being human.

Alas, politics has taken over our digital lives and with that came the greatest merger in history, and I ain't talking 'bout Instagram and Facebook.

Big Tech + Big Government = Big Problems

When internet platforms burst onto the scene, Congress offered them the same treatment as bookstores, libraries, and newsstands.

In fancy legal terms, it's what's known as the Section 230 of the Communications Decency Act and it gives platforms immunity for whatever users decide to post. So some guy tweeting a dick pic doesn't make Twitter a porn site, just like some lady sharing a CNN article on Facebook doesn't make Mark Zuckerberg a journalist. (Although, who are we kidding? No one's mistaking CNN for journalism!) These sites got this special treatment exclusively because it was assumed that they would exist as impartial channels of communication as a *platform*, not a publisher, and certainly not curators of moral authority.

Over time, however, they became emboldened to become strategic keepers of misinformation, turning the dials on suppression and amplification to their liking.

This isn't just a hunch. In 2020, the Media Research Center's Techwatch unit went through all social media posts by Trump, Biden, and their campaigns from May 2018 through October 2020. While Trump was censored a whopping sixty-five times, Biden was wholly untouched.[4] During election week, there wasn't a Trump tweet that didn't come with a disclaimer or warning if it had even gone public at all.

Yet, less than a month out from November's Election Day, Facebook and Twitter took the unprecedented step of preventing users from sharing a front-page *New York Post* story about the Biden family's dealings in Ukraine. Needless to say, it was less than flattering. Facebook announced it was (*air quotes*) "waiting on fact-checkers." Twitter gave notice that the problem was the photographs of emails posted with the story and that it didn't want to encourage potential hackers.[5]

You know what happens next. Joe Biden wins the 2020 election, and because COVID-19 dramatically altered the voting procedures in favor of mail-in ballots (plus, public distrust of American institutions is at an all-time high), many Trump supporters disputed the outcome of the election. When a group of people who believed Trump was the real victor rioted inside the US Capitol on January 6, 2021, the media along with every social media platform seized the opportunity to blow the event as far out of proportion as possible. Mainstream media outlets continue to encourage a federal investigation into the identities of those who participated—even though the violence that occurred on that day often pales in comparison to the violence that occurs nightly on the streets of cities like Portland and San Francisco.

Two days later, Facebook and Twitter permanently suspended Donald Trump's account, both personal and presidential. Instagram, YouTube, Amazon Web Services, Snapchat, Spotify, and Reddit all followed suit. Even Pinterest gave him the boot—where could Donny find apple pie recipes now?! Alas, Trump becomes a digital tramp.

A few days later, Parler, a Twitterlike platform that had hit the number-one free app on Apple, became Big Tech's new target. It had become a popular platform for a number of conservatives because it described itself as a "non-biased, free speech social media focused on protecting users' rights." By January 8, 2021, Apple and Google+ removed Parler from their app stores because they said it had not sufficiently policed its users' posts. That same weekend, Amazon Web Services completely shut down the web servers, disconnecting Parler from the internet entirely.

No matter your political leanings, totally deplatforming the sitting President of the United States and cutting off a company's access to the internet was a pivotal moment, threatening what was formerly considered the universally open internet.

Even Kate Ruane, a spokesperson for the American Civil Liberties Union (which is no defender of conservatism . . . or liberalism for that matter) noted: "We understand the desire to permanently suspend [Trump] now, but it should concern everyone when companies like Facebook and Twitter wield the unchecked power to remove people from platforms that have become indispensable for the speech of billions—especially when political realities make those decisions easier."[6]

The message in that moment was clear. If Big Tech can wipe a company off the face of the internet—if it could take out the *sitting* President of the United States—it'll eventually come for you too.

I often hear people across the political spectrum—or people who just hate Trump—say that private companies can do what they want and therefore shouldn't be subject to any regulation. The reality is that while America's founders imagined a limited government, they had no concept of a large corporation, and it never occurred to them that a business could be more powerful than the state itself. They could never have imagined that giant, global conglomerates would control all of our information and our ability to communicate with one another digitally—so the idea that corporations can do what they like is not the whole story.

It wasn't too long ago that liberals and conservatives alike wanted to battle the outsize power of the big tech corporations, fearing that over time they would start infringing on basic liberties. Which, when you actually do stop and think about our basic civil liberties— freedom of *thought*, freedom of *expression*, freedom of the *press*, freedom of *assembly*, freedom of *speech*, the right to *equal treatment* under the law, the right to *privacy*—it's easy to see how every single one of those freedoms is being violated by Big Tech. Thoughts are suppressed. Expressions are edited. Certain press is limited. Facebook groups and full platforms are banned. Speech is censored. Some are affected more by "content policy" than others. And good God almighty, do I really need to say anything about privacy?

But, per usual, it's not as cut and dry as it might seem.

On one hand, social networking sites such as Facebook and Twitter can limit, control, and censor speech more than government entities ever could. We saw how government and Big Tech coincidently came together when COVID-19 came sweeping in. The irony of strict quarantine rules was that by locking everybody in their homes for a year, social media became the primary mode of communication. By knocking people off based on political beliefs, they eventually created an echo chamber of information and opinion during the lead-up to the 2020 election.

On the other hand, for some reason I remain unconvinced that the government will ever win the battle against Big Tech. This is why we don't face a legal choice, but a moral one. Do we fight individually to retain our liberties, or do we encourage corporate power to trample on them?

Alas, social media is quite collectivist.

The moment there was content that the collective deemed bad, the Left was suddenly willing to embrace the idea of outsourcing the task of restricting those liberties. Constitutionally, daddy government can't censor us (for now) but Facebook can and progressives applaud that, and so the government allows Big Tech to do its bidding.

And, folks, I mean *literal* bidding.

Everybody knows money talks. The political donations made directly to campaigns that came from Alphabet (Google), Microsoft,

Amazon, Facebook, Twitter, and Apple soared past $50 million for the 2020 presidential election cycle, and I don't think I need to specify which campaign the bulk of it went to.[7] (Hint: it rhymes with Blow Widen.) With that, do we really think the regulations that would come from an administration funded by the very thing it's regulating isn't going to be influenced as it creates those regulations? Hmm ... me thinks not.

Ergo, Big Tech and Big Government get cozier and cozier—each equally and increasingly beholden to the other. One pours money into the other while the other provides power (although, I'm not always sure which is which).

In 2020, Amazon and Facebook were in the top ten of leading corporate spenders for DC lobbying services, spending over $38 million combined.[8] Of course, these aren't heartfelt donations; these are marketing and legal dollars spent in direct correlation to how much influence they can have on government policy. But enough about money—let's talk power.

In 2013, Amazon's Jeff Bezos bought *The Washington Post*. (Makes ya wonder: What's Citizen Jeff's rosebud?) The following year, in 2014, Amazon Web Services won a $600 million contract from the CIA.[9] Gosh, what a strange coincidence! In 2017, Amazon announced the opening of the new AWS Secret Region in which Amazon became the sole provider of cloud services across "the full range of data classifications, including Unclassified, Sensitive, Secret, and Top Secret."[10] Uh, you feeling that Big Brother gaze yet? In 2019, Amazon announced its second headquarters would be located in none other than nearby Arlington, Virginia, making the company a major employer in the DC area with over twenty-five thousand jobs to offer.[11] In just six years—from buying the hometown paper in 2013 to providing services to the CIA to employing a chunk of the DC population—Amazon managed to put a figurative stake into the swampy ground.

And what about Facebook? Well, Facebook's influence in both DC and the political landscape at large is certainly obvious. (It won't shock you to know, the guy who was in charge of election integrity was a former Biden staffer). For years Facebook has deboosted, deplatformed, amplified some voices, suppressed others, and fact-checked to the point that we may want to reconsider that ol' Section 230 of the Communications Decency Act. We already know how Facebook and social platforms in general are wildly inconsistent when upholding standards of conduct, but I'll give credit where credit's due. Despite having personally donated $400 million to campaign groups and voting infrastructure organizations, for many years Mark Zuckerberg has tried fending off calls from the Left to take even more oppressive steps toward censorship. Maybe that sprung from a true patriotic belief in free speech and open access to the internet, or maybe, *just maybe*, it was to stay in the good graces of the Trump administration for fear of regulatory actions that could cost the company big time.

Do we really think Zuckerberg's banning of Trump after four years of tension was merely due to a change of heart? Of course not, it was a change in power. Alas, a new era was introduced as Democrats took the presidency and the US House of Representatives, and goodness knows Facebook will bend over backward for them.

Ironically, when it came to what happened at the US Capitol building on January 6, 2021, most of the organizing didn't take place on Parler but rather on Facebook. In fact, even the head of the left-leaning watchdog organization Media Matters said that the Capitol raid would have still happened without Parler but not without

Facebook, arguing it had a "much bigger role" in the riot.[12] Frankly, Facebook shouldn't be blamed for what happened at the Capitol either. When someone yells fire in a crowded theater, we don't blame the owner of the theater, we blame the individual who's violated the law. But why is it that Parler exclusively took the brunt of the blame?

That one's easy. Taking out Parler had little to do with who said what where. It wasn't about doing what is right or good for society. It was about a coordinated effort—by Big Government and Big Tech— to take out the competition and garner more power.

It doesn't take a particularly paranoid mind to imagine what alliances between Big Tech and Big Government might look like, or to be frightened of where they might lead. Whether it's Amazon getting cozy with the CIA or Biden creepily stroking Facebook's backside, there is no doubt that the once-distant worlds are fast merging into a giant monstrosity, resulting in one big monopoly—technologically, politically, economically, intellectually, and culturally.

Monopoly Men

If you've ever played Monopoly, you might notice that a key way to win is to own all four railroads. There's a reason for this. The game was based on America's Gilded Age when the railroad industry totally dominated business and politics. It was kind of the Big Tech of the nineteenth century. Another way to win is to be the banker and slip yourself a little something every time someone passes Go. Consider it a government bailout!

Just like the internet, with the arrival of the railroad, time and space became obsolete—goods and people could move faster and cheaper than ever before. Suddenly, the entire nation was at the mercy of the monopolistic power of the tracks, and with no real competition, railroad companies could charge different rates to different customers. This power to decide winners and losers threatened not just independent business but also corrupted the political landscape at-large. Turns out Rich Uncle Pennybags (yes, that's really the Monopoly man's name . . . google it!) lined his pockets with more than just money.

Ironically, the term *Gilded Age* comes from a satirical novel by Mark Twain and Charles Dudley Warner titled, well, *The Gilded Age*. The novel was a less-than-flattering critique on the state of American democracy at the time, which shouldn't be all that surprising coming from Twain, who said, "Suppose you were an idiot and suppose you were a member of Congress: but I repeat myself."

Yet, with the monopolists growing in power by the day, eventually the idiots were asked to step in and pass some antitrust laws. In 1887, Congress passed the Interstate Commerce Law to regulate railroad rates and, in 1890, Congress passed the Sherman Antitrust Act to break up the monopolies. The Sherman Antitrust Act criminalized certain monopolies but didn't outlaw the possession of a monopoly altogether. When things are working well, antitrust recognizes and incentivizes investment and risk-taking. That's a good thing. The resulting competition for marketplace supremacy can be dog-eat-dog, so weaker firms may naturally fail along the way, but those that are left standing shouldn't be punished for their success. Although the antitrust laws were in this case helpful, they also introduced concerns about keeping a truly free and competitive market, and continuing to keep the government's nose out of where it shouldn't be.

Over a century later, antitrust law and policy are once again in vogue—but this time it's a train wreck. If you thought the railroad monopolies were bad, they pale in comparison to the Big Tech behemoths. So what happens when the monopoly is less about dollars and cents and more about information and common sense?

When corporate entities like Amazon, Apple, and Facebook are operating ethically and doing things right, there is little to no argument that they provide incredible, world-changing services. Who could have dreamed in Gilded Age America that we'd eventually have two-day delivery for something called a Roomba, a freaking computer in our pocket, or instant and full access to that random high school friend whose name you would've otherwise forgotten? But it's not the "operating ethically" or "doing things right" that we're worried about—it's the fear of Big Tech entities controlling our most precious resources.

Think of it like this. If Nike had a 90 percent monopoly on sneakers it would be unethical and would suck. No one wants just one choice of shoe, plus with no competition the quality would degrade over time and before we knew it, basketball players would be playing in glorified Crocs. But it wouldn't be *societally* damaging. Nike would just own the market on our feet. With Big Tech, it's got a monopoly on our minds.

Big Tech attempts to control our judgment, our reasoning, our information, and our ability to communicate. Which is why the long road to Congress that Mark Zuckerberg et al. faced from 2016 onward can be best summarized as a battle for that control: conservatives wanted government intervention to stop the banning and censoring, while liberals wanted government intervention in order to choose who to ban and censor (while libertarians were over there debating about whether or not drivers' licenses should even be legal). And while I have no particular love for Zuckerberg, you kind of felt some sympathy for the little deer caught in the headlights as you listened to members of Congress insist that he had to be the arbiter of moral authority or else they'd punish him if he couldn't figure it out correctly.

We may look back at Zuckerberg as a cunning digital tyrant; or maybe we'll just look back at him as the wee little scapegoat that the government used to outsource its oppressive desires. Who can forget on October 29, 2019, watching AOC forcefully grill him?

> **AOC:** Do you see a potential problem here with a complete lack of fact-checking on political advertisements?
>
> **Zuck:** Well, Congresswoman, I think lying is bad. And I think if you were to run an ad that had a lie, that would be bad. That's different from it being—from—in our position, the right thing to do to prevent your constituents or people in an election from seeing that you had lied.
>
> **AOC:** So, we can—so, you won't take down lies, or you will take down lies? I think this is just a pretty simple yes or no.[13]

Ruthlessly questioning to get honesty is one thing; a government agent scaring a CEO to say what she wants him to say is something else entirely. Love him or hate him, Zuckerberg's inclination was right: *I am not God.* But AOC mistook him for God, and she wanted to be the one controlling God. That's Progressive 101.

Naturally, the individualist in me says put control into the hands of the individual. Nobody is forcing me to be on YouTube. No one put a gun to my head and said, "Tweet or die!" My life won't end if I am banned from Facebook (and truth be told, one of my employees runs that page anyway). I don't want Mark Zuckerberg to have to bear the weight of every individual's posts to decide if it's factually or ethically flawless, and I don't want the CEO of Twitter to be responsible for dick pics. I want *individuals* to bear the weight of their own choices.

Look, I get it. I understand the desire for some kind of leash on Big Tech. I could even make an argument for an antitrust, if just to break up the bullies and avoid some massive societal takeover. Having a bunch of tech oligarchs—the same ones that ended the digital life of a sitting president—continue to encroach more and more on those liberties is definitely due for concern. But do we really want to hand power over to the government in a way that it could control every single bit of information we consume and every mode of communication?

It's tricky. All I know is that we always have to be wary of handing power over to the government via regulation, because we don't want Big Tech to be so institutionally wrapped up with the government— out of necessity or desire—that it becomes the new town square.

We all know that the government is notoriously bad at running *any* kind of company, let alone one involving modern technology. I mean, when's the last time you went to a government website? Do we really want our digital lives to look like AOL circa 1994? Have you ever met an interesting person at a party only to discover that the individual leads the exciting life of a government regulator? Does a creative, eccentric, entrepreneurial, trailblazing rebel come to mind? And if the people who created the damn algorithms don't even know how they work anymore, do we expect a government regulator to figure them out? To do this correctly, the government would have to hire the most ingenious technologists and programmers in the world, and do you seriously think they want to work for the government? The idea that the government could hire people competent enough to regulate Big Tech is ethically and morally deranged.

Trust me. Big government fixing a Big Tech problem would just make bigger problems.

Good news? I don't think the technology of today will (or should) last forever. I mean, when's the last time you took a steam locomotive to work? The reality is, innovations get out-innovated and these companies will eventually become so large that they can't be creative anymore. (Look at what Amazon did to Walmart.) And when you couple this reality with the fact that the most qualified engineers, programmers, and managers aren't being hired because of all that diversity and inclusion stuff, ultimately many of these companies will crumble under the weight of their own faulty policies. Trust me, the more that Big Government gets involved and decides to make technology a utility, the longer they will last—and likely far past their expiration date.

My hope is that today's social media expires quickly. I hope someone will build an entirely new internet and that someday soon we'll look back at our current state of social media and think, *My god, did we really talk to one another that way? Did we really lose our ability to discern to that extent?* Because although it's easy to point the finger at Facebook or even Mark Zuckerberg himself, it just simply isn't fair. The current state of our public discourse is ugly because *we* made it that way. We're addicted to shock and awe; we love watching the provocative drama of our digital world unfold in our pajamas. Information monopolists, like Facebook and Amazon, just gave us what we wanted, making billions along the way and leaving us ripe for top-down manipulation and control. This wasn't an accident, folks; it's just a part of the game of Monopoly.

Keep It Local

I'll let you in on a little secret.

Soon after we had decided to take what I had created post-Patreon to the public, I popped into a little wine shop. Anyone who's ever had to name anything—albeit a business, a book, or a baby—knows that there's a constant search for inspiration. You're always waiting for something to jump out and inspire you to better encapsulate everything you want to say in just a word or two. Despite all the wine, it was fairly fruitless. Finally I got to the aisle of reds and noticed a bottle of pinot noir named "Sea Stack."

I suddenly thought of PayPal founder Peter Thiel, who I've had on *The Rubin Report* and has since become a good friend of mine. He was very into the idea of seasteading, the concept of building floating societies that, in effect, could exist as libertarian utopias in the sea. It was rooted in the idea that nearly half of the world's surface is unclaimed by any nation-state, so building autonomous, futuristic islands, or seasteads, could solve problems like overpopulation, poor governance, and too many creative restraints.[14] It had risen in popularity for a while, but eventually drifted off (no pun intended).

Seasteading was more of an imaginative thought experiment than a reality, ultimately posing and answering the question: If you could design your own country from scratch, what would it look like?

As I stood surrounded by cabernets and zinfandels, it hit me; I immediately felt that Seastead Digital would be the perfect name for what I was trying to do. I wanted to swim against the tide. I wanted to create a place of creative freedom and digital autonomy, where each person could create their own customized community floating on the technological waves of the internet. I wanted individuals to establish their own terms and conditions and actually *own* the content that they shared with those they decided to share it with.

So there ya go. The secret's out. Before Locals was Locals, it was Seastead Digital. Fortunately, one of our original investors owned the domain name locals.com and it was just too perfect to pass up—because when faced with the overreach of Big Tech and Big Government, the only thing that can really save us is our *local* communities.

Most of us just want to live our lives privately and care about our loved ones and the people around us. The problem is we're going to have this ever-encroaching movement of people who want to control our lives from afar. Locals was my attempt to bring the sanity back to the public forum on a digital level and to bring the "social" back into social media. I promise, you don't have to hate your aunt Verna. You don't have to fight with that friend from high school about something happening in a state neither of you live in. You don't have to scroll through your newsfeed to zoom past baby pictures, then terrorist-attack alerts, then a puppy, then a conspiracy theory. Our whole cognitive way of being is getting knocked out because of Big Tech. Maybe that's by design and maybe it's not and it's just the way humans are. Either way, I think taking control of your digital life is the key to not letting our inherent humanity slip away.

Remember, technology is like a fire—it can warm up a home and it can burn it down. So when the technological powers grab hold of your life, just be a little more human. Use that natural human ingenuity to make new things and build the businesses and institutions of the future. We were meant for more than to just complain and do nothing. We are social creatures meant to build and create. We are meant to be participants in the game being played, not just stagnant Monopoly board-game pieces.

After the Big Government giant joins forces with the Big Tech beast, it won't be long until we'll have a radioactive, algorithmically boosted monster on our hands. But David beat Goliath and we can too. Because if we don't stand up against them, nobody will, and then this whole game—this whole beautiful game about freedom on the internet, will all be over just as it started.

And if I've been deleted by YouTube by the time this book is published, you can find me at rubinreport.locals.com.

5

EMBRACE YOUR INNER BLACK SHEEP

"People should not fear their governments.
Governments should fear their people."

Alan Moore, *V for Vendetta*

Pulling the Wool

Adolf Hitler (who was a real, you know, *actual* Nazi) hated germs.

He was said to have bathed four times a day, called himself an *einsiedler*, literally translating to "insider," meaning recluse or hermit, and he was repulsed by sex for fear of catching STDs (or maybe that's cause he was rumored to have had just one ball).[1] As Hitler rose to power, it seems he was very concerned with the hygiene of the German people.

In fact, his first policy implementation was tuberculosis screenings. He sent out fleets of vans to x-ray everyone and rid Germany of tuberculosis. Of course, there was little pushback—no one likes TB!

Then the Nazis started cleaning up the factories. They came in and sprayed Zyklon B in all the nooks and crannies to get rid of all the nasty rats and bugs and began planting beautiful flowers out front. No one could dispute a beautification campaign. How could you? It's beautiful!

But Hitler's purity campaign extended, bit by bit, and eventually he would use Zyklon B to kill millions of Jews—that same gas he used to kill the rats and bugs.

In a 2017 lecture titled, "Biology and Traits: Orderliness/Disgust/Conscientiousness," Jordan Peterson put it like this: "People think of [Nazi Germany] as descent into barbarity, but what it looks like is a disease of civilization." The world Hitler rose to power in was a chaotic one to say the least. The aftermath of WWI and the devastation brought on by Spanish influenza left the Germans desperate for order. This desperation made them ripe for order of any kind, no matter how extreme or overreaching. So the German people were psychologically prepared, therefore, to fall in line with a uniformed, "civilized," organized, and controlling regime.[2]

But as it turns out, the correlation between infectious diseases and the degree to which authoritarian beliefs are held is not specific to Hitler and Nazism. Jordan went on to pose an interesting question and even more interesting answer: "How do you fight authoritarian governments across the world? You get rid of infectious disease."

Jordan's reply was in response to a 2013 study by Damian R. Murray, Mark Schaller, and Peter Suedfeld in which they unpacked something called "parasite stress." It's the idea that authoritarian governments are more likely to emerge in regions characterized by a high predominance of disease-causing pathogens. *I think you know where I am going with this....*

According to the theory, people who live in areas with higher rates

of parasites are more likely to think and behave in ways that minimize their risk of infection and increase their risk for being abused
under authoritarianism.

The study opens with this:

> Systems of governance differ widely, and one important dimen-
> sion on which they vary is authoritarianism. In contrast to lib-
> eral democratic forms of governance (characterized by popular
> participation in the political process, and by protection of in-
> dividual civil rights and ideological freedoms), authoritarian
> governance is defined by highly concentrated power structures
> that repress dissent and emphasize submission to authority, so-
> cial conformity, and hostility towards outgroups.[3]

The first study was conducted in thirty-one countries where
empirical data was available for (a) authoritarian governance, (b) individual authoritarianism, and (c) historical prevalence of disease-
causing parasites. The second study zeroed in on smaller cultural
populations—ninety to be exact. What the researchers found was
pretty damn mind-boggling. Turns out, a countrywide survey
showed it was consistent with the idea that with large numbers of
disease come authoritarian beliefs. (The actual rate ends up being
about 0.70, which is a higher correlation than between IQ and
grades—that's to say it's pretty high.[4]) Results revealed that with
higher prevalence of infectious pathogens, comes higher likelihood
for authoritarian governance, and did so even when intentionally
comparing it to other threats to human welfare, including famine,
malnutrition, and warfare (the latter, oddly, had the least correlation).

The study's researchers also concluded that individuals who perceive the threat of infectious disease tend to become more *conformist*. "Because many disease-causing parasites are invisible, and their actions mysterious, disease control has historically depended substantially on adherence to ritualized behavioral practices that reduce infection risk."[5] Think face masks, six-feet distance, 9:00 p.m. curfews, stay-at-home orders, quarantine mandates. Any time there is risk of infection, certain people prefer unquestioned obedience to authority and respond negatively to people who fail to conform. In other words, they become collectivists and shun individualists.

History and information teach us a couple things here:

First, where there is a contagion, there is an opportunity to gain control: *stay home, wear that, and do this because you don't know what's good for you but we as the authorities do.*

Second, where disease runs rampant, fear runs *high*. It's a savior complex at its finest—so, rather than quell the fear, the "savior" stokes it, creating an infectious codependency of citizens relying on the government.

Think of it like this: Moms everywhere admit that they experience the tiniest bit of joy when their child experiences some small-scale suffering—say a bad dream, a skinned knee, or a teenage breakup. Why? Not because moms are unempathetic, sociopathic monsters (at least most of them aren't) but because the child comes running to them seeking that comfort only a mother can give, and suddenly, the mother feels *needed*. Of course, that kind of behavior can lead to more serious forms of codependency if left unchecked, and similarly, a group of citizens can be crippled and dependent on authority to make choices on their behalf—choices that aren't a government's job to make.

Remember, folks, the study results were published in 2013. It would be another seven years until COVID-19 would come in hot. Jordan gave that lecture in 2017, and yet it resonates now more than ever.

The threat and the fear confined people. It caused people to conform and fall in line with strange behavioral practices and unquestioned obedience. (Should we wash our grocery bags? Should we wear two masks, just to play it safe? Should we hide under our beds until Lord Fauci says it's safe to come out?) The fear distanced us from one another at a great cost to economies and personal well-being. And the pressure grew and grew for large institutions to do something—anything—to stop it.

There's an old saying, *never let a crisis go to waste.* For authoritarian-leaning leaders worldwide, the COVID-19 pandemic was the crisis they had been dreaming of. It gave them an opportunity to push oppressive restrictions and laws to repress independent voices in society—all under the guise of asserting that an unprecedented crisis requires unprecedented measures.

Nowhere was the power grab more obvious than in Moscow, where ol' Vladimir Putin announced he would be president until 2036—or translated from the original Russian into layman's English: *forever.*[6] For months leading up to the pandemic, a delicate dance was going to pass complex constitutional amendments that would restructure the Russian government so Vlad could remain the central political force in the country.[7] Despite an unenthused public's reaction to the referendum that mostly just highlighted his very personal ideologies, he referenced—wait for it—COVID-19 as the reason why there needs to be stability at the top of government.[8]

Hmm. How convenient.

The Russian government also stepped up its surveillance capabilities during that time to enforce a quarantine for, you know, the *safety* of its citizens. With 178,000 facial-recognition cameras in Moscow at the time—and plans to install thousands more in the following months—the government also focused on advancements in facial recognition software to catch individuals breaking the lockdown restrictions. But it didn't end there. Operations to monitor social media for spreading false information about the outbreak was put into place as well.[9]

"But that's just Russia being Russia, Dave!"

Clearly, it wasn't just Russia or that other big authoritarian government in China either. Efforts to stabilize the virus led to abuse of civil liberties here on our own turf.

At the beginning of the pandemic, it was *stay home for two weeks to "flatten the curve."* Totally doable! Everyone can come together for a couple of weeks to try to get our heads around what seemed to be a legitimately scary contagion. But those two weeks turned into two months, which turned into six months, which turned into a year, which turned to two years and, well, you get the idea. Suddenly, no one was talking about "flattening the curve" and strict quarantine laws just kept getting enforced even if the curve was flattened. (Can anyone really tell me if the thing got flat? Did it morph into a squiggle? Did it mutate into a doodle? I don't know.) The line between science and propaganda eventually blurred, and restrictions were doled out—for traveling, for celebrating Thanksgiving, for going to the beach—without any justifications for them. I mean, can anyone explain to me why all Los Angeles beaches were closed throughout almost half of 2020? It didn't make sense then, but we were all in a state of shock, so I'll cut us some slack. In retrospect, it was all bullshit from the beginning.

I was totally shocked at the way the average American just took orders as time wore on—most people didn't even seem to ask *why* these things were happening or whether the efforts were actually working. Pretty much everyone basically fell in line and fully complied.

Instead of projecting certainty that we could conquer COVID, as President Donald Trump did by encouraging the use of over-the-counter remedies like hydroxychloroquine, our COVID czars focused on capitalizing on the chaos—preparing for a forever pandemic. For instance, Apple and Google announced in April 2020 that millions of phones around the world got a new feature to help track and slow down the spread of coronavirus called "contact tracing" and gave users the option to receive "exposure notifications." Although the actual developers of those apps and other similar tracking devices may have had good intentions, as we know, the road to hell is paved with 'em.

Crises create an opportunity for those at the helm—government, Big Tech, the mainstream media—to strengthen their grip and tighten the noose. When the COVID-19 outbreak made landfall, it presented a unique combination of circumstances that were ripe for leaders' megalomania. With fears at an all-time high, people were more than happy to obey and conform to whatever far-reaching rules and restrictions the government enforced. People wanted the kind of nationwide response that only mommy government can provide—and so we tripped, skinned our knees, and went desperately running to whom we thought could save us, no questions asked.

Well, some of us still have questions.

A Pew Research Center survey, reported on October 21, 2020—months after the initial lockdown and a couple weeks before the 2020 election—found that only 24 percent of conservative voters found the coronavirus outbreak a very important factor when casting their vote during the 2020 general election. A whopping 82 percent of Democrat-leaning voters said that the coronavirus outbreak was a very important factor for their vote during the 2020 general election, blaming Trump for a less aggressive response. The irony? The same people who were calling Trump a tyrant were angry that he had not exercised his federal power by implementing tyrannical safety measures.

Only in a very sick system could a virus originating over seven thousand miles away become so politically infectious.

Why, you ask? The first answer should be obvious—conspicuously hiding in the very real epidemic of partisan polarization. Because at the heart of contemporary partisanship is the ability for polarization to change reality, enabling political affiliation to determine what you think is happening around you—at least for the non-thinking individual. But we already know this.

The second answer is a bit trickier to deconstruct. Is it that bleeding-heart liberals are more concerned for the health of others and just happen to know more family members or friends that got infected? Was it that conservatives just hate science? Are conservatives greedy lovers of capitalism who prioritize business over human suffering?

Nah, no, and nope.

Conservatives guarded their autonomy while everyone else offered up their freedom to Fauci on a silver platter.

Black Sheep

After not traveling for eight months, my first trip was to the exotic land of Dallas, Texas, to visit Mercury Studios to sit with Glenn Beck in his home for a Blaze Media taping.

We sat down one on one. Nothing in particular on the agenda to discuss, although I was selfishly hoping to take a break from the detailed minutiae of daily updates around the 2020 general election or whatever new requirements the CDC was announcing for the holiday season.

As we sat down, I saw that Glenn was eagerly holding a stack of files and papers, ready to get the conversation going. Moments in, I was thankful that the headline du jour was not on the menu. Instead, he decided he wanted to go through some of his most prized possessions among his vast collection of historical documents—letters from *the* George Washington and original notes that Thomas Jefferson made on the Declaration of Independence.

Midway into the conversation Glenn held up one of the papers in his hand.

"This one my wife gave to me for Christmas. She didn't want to give it to me on Christmas Day." She knew if she did, he'd be preoccupied with it for the rest of the day.

It was a document printed by Raoul Wallenberg, a Swedish diplomat in Budapest during World War II, who was responsible for saving the lives of tens of thousands of Jews, though many put that number at over one hundred thousand.

Glenn went on to describe the document, "What it says is, 'This woman now belongs to my kingdom. This woman doesn't have to wear your yellow star and she's a *Swedish* citizen.'"

Wallenberg was tireless when distributing the documents. He would stand in front of trains en route to death camps, and if they stopped, he would climb atop the cars and stuff as many papers as he could between the slats of the train, shouting, "Everybody grab hold of one of these. *Everyone* take hold of one of these!" Then he would run to the front of the train and demand that the Jewish prisoners be released as individuals under Swedish protection.

His remarkable bravery also applied in the diplomatic arena. Wallenberg is said to have bribed, bullied, and threatened German and Hungarian leaders into halting or delaying deportations, working round the clock to find a way to save as many Jews as he could before they continued.

According to Wallenberg, "To me there's no other choice. I've accepted this assignment and I could never return to Stockholm without the knowledge that I'd done everything in human power to save as many Jews as possible."[10]

Eventually, Wallenberg disappeared. The official Soviet account, issued in 1957, was that he died of a heart attack at thirty-four years old. Few take that account seriously, however. Most people believe that Soviet jailers abducted him and executed him.[11]

On Glenn's desk, beside pictures of his wife and kids, is a small black and white picture of young Raoul Wallenberg. On days he needs an extra dose of inspiration, he looks toward Raoul's impact on history to drum it up in himself.

Here's the thing. Brave, nonconforming, courageous people don't suddenly become courageous when they need to be—they simply refuse to go over the cliff when the rest of humanity walks off of it.

They question the "facts," they ask, "Why?" They remain grounded in the lessons history has taught us time and time and time again. Because we always seem to forget that the road off the cliff is incremental: *test for TB, spray the rats with Zyklon B, create a "clean" society.*

You don't have to be superhuman to have courage, you just have to be willing to stand up for what you believe.

When I was on tour with Jordan Peterson, one of the things that often came up in his lectures at some point is this: "There are three thousand of you sitting there, and I guarantee every single one of you would think you wouldn't be a Nazi if this was 1936 Germany, but that proves that every single one of you probably would have been."

We all *think* we would do the right thing—that we would resist the powers that be and protect individuals against the machine even if it was unpopular—but, if faced with that reality, would we really?

Courage takes preparation. Bravery takes a deep sense of pre-drawn lines that if crossed becomes your internal wake-up call to do something about it.

If I would have told you in 2019 that the government would shut down the economy and say you can't have Thanksgiving with your family and you have to wear a mask all the time, you would have probably thought I was crazy. You might think: *Well, maybe the government making personal decisions about how I spend my time with my family is a good line for me to draw in the sand?* But it became normal—a *new normal.*

What happens to a society when those in power cross a small line and then another and then another and then another? What happens to a group of individuals who fail to think for themselves, fail to ask good questions and merely follow the route of the collective? You'll wake up to find yourself doing things you never dreamt you'd do.

You'll find yourself doing things not because they make sense but because, well, you were simply told to. (Two masks anybody? Three?)

When it came to COVID-19, let's just all come out and say it: the science was always secondary (and a little bit sketchy). Diseases don't have schedules, so why were 9 p.m. curfews enforced? Infections don't have shopping preferences, so why could Target and Walmart stay open while small mom-and-pop shops had to close down? Some data showed that wearing masks helped, while others said it did little, and others said it was actually harmful because you touch your face more when wearing masks. So were the masks protective of our health or protective of our egos, as symbols of collective conformity (or as Rand Paul put it, as just "theater"[12])?

You've probably heard of the famous Asch Conformity Experiments, when Solomon Asch investigated how social pressure from a majority could cause an individual to conform. The tests consisted of eight people all lined up—seven who were in on the experiment and one noob who knew nothing. The experimenter would go to each person, one at a time, and show them a card, asking the person to choose which of the three lines on the left card matched the length of the line on the right card. The task was repeated several times with different cards, but on every single card the answer was painfully (and I mean *painfully*) obvious.

When the seven intentionally gave the wrong answer, the other guy would conform. Over the twelve trials, about 75 percent of participants conformed at least one time. In the control group, however, where there was no pressure to conform, less than 1 percent of participants gave the wrong answer. (Gee, what's their problem?) In the end, Asch concluded that people conform because they want to fit in with the group and because they believe the majority is always right.[13]

But that's when you truly find yourself among a majority—what's even more fascinating is that our current woke collective isn't a majority at all; its members are just loud enough to cleverly trick us into thinking it's more than just a small fraction.

But there's another interesting conclusion from the study.

When an individual stands up against the group, he observed a strong activation in the amygdala, a part of the brain closely associated with fear.[14] The amygdala response disappears when others—or even just one—speak up. In other words, one person standing up for what was *true* was all it took to lessen this fear response and compel others to do the same.

The more I have come out of my political closet over the years, the more I think about the ol' adage, "The only thing to fear is fear itself." Now that I've been promoting unpopular opinions for a few years, the more I believe that statement to be true. The more I say things that may not be trendy but are truthful, the less fearful I am to say other important things. I just have to keep standing up for what I believe in consistently. No matter how scary. It's like a muscle, and I've built it up to the point that I barely feel fear at all anymore. Though the ending of *The Blair Witch Project* still freaks me out.

This is also why it's important to know and be educated about *why* you do what you do. Hold on to those convictions and values. The more prepared about these decisions you can be ahead of time, the less likely you are to be controlled when the winds of conformity blow in strong and swift.

Dr. Christopher D. Frith, professor of neuroscience at University College, London, and experimental psychologist Daniel Campbell-Meiklejohn of the University of Sussex, also studied the links between the brain and conformity. In one of their studies they concluded that when we're in agreement with others, our brains show increased activity in their reward center.

In one study, researchers mapped participants' ratings of music, and the subjects were then shown what music critics had thought of that same music. Using functional MRI, investigators discovered that the lateral orbitofrontal cortex (the part of the brain associated with emotion, reward, and decision-making) became active, as most participants switched or corrected their selections to conform with the critics' ratings. Dr. Frith said, "The ability to adapt to others and align ourselves with them is an important social skill [and] social conformation is, at least in part, hardwired in the structure of the brain."[15]

Anyone looking to control you knows how to use this information for their benefit. With carrots on sticks, conformity is rewarded, and conversely, punishment meted out to those that go against the grain.

The sad part is they don't even need to. People's natural desire to conform is mental reward enough—good comrades know that they can enforce the rules themselves. Which is why authoritarian governments love for us to follow the rules without asking why—the collective can get the job done with little to no input.

Hannah Arendt, the German-born American political philosopher, famously argued that the atrocities of the Holocaust were not caused by psychopaths but by ordinary people placed under pressure to conform. In her words, "Evil comes from a failure to think. It defies thought for as soon as thought tries to engage itself with evil and examine the premises and principles from which it originates, it is frustrated because it finds nothing there. That is the banality of evil."

Arendt is talking particularly about the war crimes of Adolf Eichmann, the Nazi operative responsible for organizing the transportation of millions of Jews to concentration camps.

Eichmann was ordinary. In her words, "neither perverted nor sadistic" but "terrifyingly normal."

Eichmann wasn't the devil; he was just a sheep.

Follow the Leader

It was a typical morning in 2005 on a farm in Istanbul, Turkey. The farmers went to have breakfast as the sheep grazed. Looking up between sips of coffee, they watched as one sheep walked off a cliff, followed by another and another, followed by eleven hundred more. More than four hundred sheep initially died. Those that jumped last had the dead sheep to break their fall.[16]

It's not that sheep are stupid, it's that they are just hardwired to follow the sheep in front of them. So when one sheep decides to go somewhere—albeit over a cliff or to slaughter—the others are likely to join.

Which is why a wolf isn't the most dangerous predator to sheep. A wolf is obvious. Its intentions and motives are clear. There's an animal much more nefarious, much more cunning, and much more performative: a goat.

A "Judas" goat is a trained goat used to herd animals. Because sheep have a habit of following any herd member that seems to know where to go, and the goat grazes with the herd and otherwise behaves as if it is a member of the herd, it becomes accepted by the herd. At the designated time, this goat's job is to lead the sheep to slaughter while its own life is spared. The Judas goat may even get a treat for it.

Holy sheep shit, does this ring a bell.

Politics consist of many a Judas goat not living by the same set of rules they demand of their sheep.

I'll amend, ever so slightly, radio broadcaster Edward R. Murrow's quote: *A nation of sheep will beget a government of Judas goats.*

Take House Speaker Nancy Pelosi, who supported strict COVID-19 lockdowns and advocated for a national mask policy. A month into the lockdowns, she appeared via livestream on CBS's *Late Late Show*, during which she showed James Corden her elaborate ice cream collection while standing in front of high-end, twin Sub-Zero fridges filled to the brim with ice cream. This was when people were fearing for the future of their livelihoods and facing economic turmoil while also going stir-crazy from quarantine. As a political leader, this was a "let them eat cake" moment. If Pelosi really believed all the things she was saying about the COVID-19 pandemic, would she really find it appropriate to show off her lavish ice cream collection? Remember, she's supposed to be a leader, not a celebrity.

But it gets worse. Months later she was caught mid-pandemic dropping into a hair salon in San Francisco (which was ordered closed by Governor Gavin Newsom—more on that asshat in a bit). The salon's camera showed her walking around without a mask despite blasting Trump for giving a speech in front of a live audience. Guys. You don't get it. She *really* needed a blowout. A few days later, instead of owning up, she took the Judas goat approach. It was the *salon's* fault. She claimed that she had been set up: "I take responsibility for trusting the word of the neighborhood salon that I've been to over the years many times, and when they said, 'We're able to accommodate people one person at a time,' I trusted that," the Speaker said. "So I take responsibility for falling for a setup. And that's all I'm going to say on that. I think that this salon owes me an apology for setting me up."

You'd never guess it, but the salon owner, Erica Kious, had a different story and responded to Pelosi's claim on *Tucker Carlson Tonight*. Kious said the idea that she set Pelosi up was "absolutely false." She went on to vent her frustrations fairly. "She's been coming in for quite a while, and just to see her come in and especially not wearing the mask, that's what really got to me, but this isn't even political. . . . It's the fact that she actually came in and didn't have a mask on. . . . And I just thought about, you know, my staff and people not being able to work and make money and provide for their families, and if she's in there comfortably without a mask and feeling safe, then why are we shut down? Why am I not able to have clients come in?"[17]

Couldn't have said it better myself.

And what about ol' Commander Newsom of California? He broke all the rules he himself set when he met up with a crowd of maskless lobbyists and politicians at the ridiculously expensive French Laundry, dropping a cool $15,000 on the alcohol bill alone. That salmon tartare amuse-bouche must be real tasty—tasty enough that San Francisco mayor, London Breed, did the same damn thing.

Predictably, the list of lefty politicians not listening to their own rules is long.

After enforcing incredibly harsh protocols on restaurants and shops, Denver mayor Michael B. Hancock flew to Mississippi to spend Thanksgiving with his family after urging others to stay home. The mayor of Austin, Steve Adler, traveled to Cabo San Lucas, Mexico . . . on a private jet . . . after hosting a wedding for twenty.

Chicago mayor Lori Lightfoot yelled maskless into a bullhorn at a celebratory rally for Biden's victory. Days later she tweeted, "Wear a mask. Listen to Science" in response to the surge of cases in Illinois.

This last example hits closer to home. Los Angeles County Supervisor Sheila Kuehl was seen eating outdoors at Il Forno Trattoria in Santa Monica just *hours* after voting to ban outdoor dining in L.A. That next day I went over to her house. To protest.

Sure, politicians ain't politicians without displaying a little bit of hypocrisy and tone-deaf greed, but during a pandemic that forced the nation into isolation and left millions without paychecks, it felt personal. It wasn't funny; people's lives were being destroyed.

This isn't a monarchy or a dictatorship where those in charge are expected to have special perks over those they control. This isn't a theocracy in which people make sacrifices at the altar of their leader. This is a democracy, where leaders are meant to represent the people, not act in ways that suggest they're above the people that elected them, enforcing oppressive laws that they fail to follow themselves.

We currently have a political class who wants to operate one way—getting haircuts and dining at five-star world-class restaurants—while others have to scrounge for survival. That is not a good recipe for a functioning society.

The Left's ability to talk about how morally righteous they are without actually *doing* any of the follow-through, is virtue signaling at its finest: *I'll say the right things, but do nothing right. I may look like a good little sheep, but trust me, I am no mutton and I'll do what I want.*

Judas goats are hypocrites at best and sociopaths at worst. They may look the part, but their goal isn't to die alongside the sheep. It's to dangerously lead and get off scot-free. I guess all animals are equal, just some are more equal than others. (Hey, no one told me there was a sequel to *Animal Farm!*)

Alas, this is what happens when the sheep just keep on following the Judas goat leaders. We create the world we live in, so remember: every time you vote, you are voting for the things that the government *shouldn't* do. Keep your intrinsic liberties at the forefront of your mind, and keep any kind of authoritarian powers—whether it comes from the Left or from the Right—in check.

This is why it's all the more important to have a philosophical, not partisan, compass to steer by—principles that hold true even in *unprecedented* times.

When individuality, autonomy, and unique thought is at the center of your worldview, suddenly the partisanship melts away. Best of all, you fight off the strange need to be politically performative for your party of choice's sake. You don't follow the leader because it's simply easier and more rewarding to conform and not ask questions (I promise it's neither in the long run), but instead prioritize free thought over political obedience.

Fellow black sheep: Inform yourself. Think for yourself. Do it yourself. Because the only way to combat collectivist conformity is to, well, not simply follow the herd.

Or you can live like a sheep being led to slaughter. Your call.

6

YOU DON'T NEED A BUNKER (BUT YOU DO NEED A PLAN)

"If you strike me down, I shall become more powerful than you can possibly imagine."

Obi-Wan Kenobi

The Weight of Wellness

Before I moved to freedom-loving Florida, I lived in fad-loving Los Angeles, and there is not a day that goes by where you don't overhear a conversation about the newest wellness trend: goat yoga, jade vagina eggs, juice cleansing, sound bathing, you name it. Whether you want to lose weight, gain weight, look younger, look older, be more present, or detach yourself from the stresses of the day, there is a new fad for you that is endorsed by literally no trusted sources.

Everyone wants to be happier and healthier. Then why—despite our human progress and the worldwide popularity of the wellness movement's journey to becoming a $4.5 trillion industry[1]—have we gotten fatter, more stressed out, uglier, and depressed?

Around the world, obesity rates are climbing—there are now more than 2 billion people considered overweight or obese. That's a third of the world's population.[2] The last two decades have resulted in a huge spike in adult acne.[3] Depressive symptoms are on the rise in just about everyone. There's been a 30 percent increase in the rate of death by suicide in the United States between 2000 and 2016.[4] This doesn't even include the spike in suicides during the COVID-19 pandemic.

Wait a minute. Shouldn't your Peloton be fixing all this? And what about your gluten-free diet? Is your meditation podcast not doing the trick? Are all these silent retreats not working or what?

In 2020, many people found themselves with more time on their hands than ever before. The lockdowns forced us inward, literally and figuratively. When life as we knew it ended, many turned to sharing positive affirmations via memes on Instagram, smoking every meat known to man, or allowing themselves to binge-watch Netflix morning to night. Should we be all that surprised when months later we were sadder, still stressed, and thirty pounds heavier?

The reality is we don't need self-care; we need self-reliance. We don't need self-love; we need self-sufficiency.

It was that summer of 2020 that David and I decided to take stock of how dependent we were on the world outside. If the grocery stores all shut down, could we find food? Could we defend our home against an intruder? Were we prepared and healthy enough to survive if our physical wellness was put to the test? (There are bears in California.) Hell, if our typical modes of fun and enjoyment were taken away from us—even things as simple as going for a walk with the dog— could we still feel happy?

When the world has made so much progress it's easy to become dependent on those forms of progress. Most people don't produce anything for themselves, nor do they know how to. We work for money to buy the things we want or need. If hungry, you buy a sandwich; if thirsty, you get a glass of water; if a tire pops, you call roadside assistance; if lost, you open Google Maps.

We assume that the system will take care of us—and when that system is working, it does a pretty okay job—but what about when the system fails? What about when people lose jobs and fight over food and supplies? Can we really be certain that the system will stay afloat and the government can save us simply by printing more money?

So, we started with the obvious: we stocked up on some nonperishable foods. Crisis or not it feels good to open up the pantry doors and see shelves filled with food. We bought the standard soup, beans, and protein bars, and our pantry overfloweth with canned tuna. If the zombie apocalypse ever does come, I'm going to die of a mercury overdose long before the zombies would ever even get to me . . . and if they did, then the zombie will probably die of a mercury overdose, because I think mercury passes through.

We also bought a Berkey water filter so that if the water went out, I could just walk on down to the Los Angeles River and turn the radioactive city sludge into drinking water.

Then we moved on to greener pastures. Literally. We planted a garden—strawberries, tomatoes, peppers, cabbage—the whole shebang. We went out and got dirt and planters and seeds and tended to them. Now, each day we're enjoying the literal fruits of our labor. Suddenly, we felt a little less reliant on the system and a little bit more reliant on ourselves. Plus all that natural vitamin D didn't hurt.

Once the pantry was packed, the plants were planted, and our emergency hydration was taken care of, we moved on to the next issue: we bought some guns.

Yep, we were among the 5 million Americans who bought a gun for the first time in 2020.[5] In just seven months—from March through September 2020—Americans bought 15.1 million firearms, a 91 percent jump from the same period in 2019.[6] Congrats to all the progressives who wanted to defund the police while simultaneously telling everyone that they were coming for their guns! You did a great job of causing gun sales.

Mainstream likes to paint the picture that it's right-wing nutjobs running to the gun shows in their cutoffs and camos, but that just isn't the case. The increase in sales was surprisingly bipartisan—sales increased across the political spectrum in 2020. People feared for their personal safety, and suddenly, with doomsday drawing nearer, they wanted to take action. (Even some of my well-known Hollywood friends bought guns that year, although they'd shoot me if I named names.)

It's kind of like the Prepper Movement. For decades, people have called them crazy, radical, weirdos. Now, most if not all of us have taken on at least *some* of their habits (if at some point you bought more than your normal amount of toilet paper or booze I am looking at you). But, really, who's the crazy one? The guy who waited for the government to end the pandemic or the self-sufficient, thoughtful, prepared guy? After years and years of the government failing to do much successfully, some people were just smart enough to take things into their own hands.

But even before the outbreak of COVID-19, preparing for emergencies was on the rise. A 2013 study estimated that 3.7 million Americans actively identify as preppers or survivalists.[7] In 2017 a survey found that roughly 20 percent of Americans spent money on survival materials that year, and 27 percent said they already had what they needed for an emergency. In 2020 it jumped to 115.6 million Americans—that's roughly half the nation's population.[8]

The driving force for preparedness isn't paranoia; it's the desire to be able to live life without worries. (I think I even read somewhere that it bothers some people when their city is burning down and a violent mob is marching in front of their house.) Preparedness, self-reliance, and self-sufficiency allow us to live more confidently and happily so we can stay physically and mentally fit and focus on the things we want to do, rather than to just worry about headlines and what could happen if we fail to prepare properly.

The goal of owning a gun or even a bunker is to *not* have to use it. It's also the same reason that you keep a fire extinguisher on hand or keep a spare tire in your trunk—ideally your home *doesn't* catch fire and you *don't* pop a tire in the middle of nowhere. But fires happen and there are nails in the road—having that extinguisher and spare tire (and knowing how to use them) can save your life when a firefighter or car mechanic can't respond in time, let alone your witch-doctor shaman from that one wellness trip you took two years ago.

We have a tendency to turn outward for everything. We ask "experts" for advice. We expect the government to solve all our problems. We use drugs when we're in pain. We expect our partners to make us happy. Worst of all, we're shocked to the point of self-destruction when those things fail us. We get more depressed, we get more dependent, and we experience more pain.

A key to surviving and thriving is cultivating confidence about what you are capable of. It feels good to not be overly dependent and have tangible skills. It feels good to garden and to be able to protect your family. It feels good to hear about the approaching winter storm or worldwide pandemic and not have to make a last last-minute run to the grocery to stockpile whatever remains in the frozen-food section because you know you already have enough supplies at home. It feels good to pop a tire yet not feel nervous if someone can't save you in a timely manner, or at all—to be able to simply hop out of your car and fix the situation, calmly and assuredly. It feels good to spend time learning how to be a living, breathing, fully functioning autonomous person who need not feel so worried about your day-to-day.

Plus I'm guessing it's cheaper than a jade vagina egg or silent retreat. Because while trendy fads only last for a minute, self-reliance lasts a lifetime.

The Art of Self-Reliance

One summer day in Boston, Massachusetts, a young Christian minister stepped in front of his congregation at the Second Unitarian Church. He'd only been teaching there for two years but was ready to move on. He had become disillusioned—so he resigned from his job, moved, abandoned his hefty family endowment, and set out to pursue his own theology. Years later he would become one of the most recognized and beloved writers in American literature.

Ralph Waldo Emerson was an individualist through and through. In 1841, he wrote his most well-known essay, "Self-Reliance." Within it, Emerson defines individualism as a deep and unshakeable trust in one's own intuitions. (This is where commands like "Trust thyself" and phrases such as "It's not the destination, it's the journey" came from.) Ironically, Emerson was in some ways the founder of the self-love movement we're living in now. When you hear that Insta-gram influencer tell you that *you can change your way of thinking, you can change your reality*, that, my friend, isn't a yoga instructor's af-firmations, it's Ralph Waldo Emerson.

The main idea in "Self-Reliance" is that the greatest things of value don't come from outward institutions—they come from within. The essay is also his most comprehensive writing for one of his most re-peated themes: the need for each individual to avoid conformity and instead follow his own instincts:

> "Society everywhere is in conspiracy against the manhood of every one of its members. Society is a joint-stock company, in which the members agree, for the better securing of his bread to each shareholder, to surrender the liberty and culture of the eater. The virtue in most request is conformity. Self-reliance is its aversion. It loves not realities and creators, but names and customs."[9]

In other words, if you aren't solely reliant on yourself—your own body and your own brain—you're eventually going to become reliant on something else. Emerson didn't leave the church because he was anti-*God*. He left the church because he was anti-institution. Histor-ically, institutions such as the government, the church, and academia use the structure itself to shape people and society. True men—true humans—are individualists or, in Emerson's words, "Whoso would be a man, must be a nonconformist."[10]

The moment your reliance is fixed on something other than your-self, is the moment you conform and, like Emerson writes later in the essay, "imitation is suicide." It's the total loss of self. I mean, how can you trust thyself, love thyself, or care for thyself if you don't have a self at all?

It's kind of like the ol' saying: give a man a fish and you feed him for a day, teach a man to fish and you feed him for a lifetime.

This is the abundance and *true* progress that was envisioned by our nation's founders. When each individual has the ability to go fishing, he or she doesn't have to rely on the fishy government. A limited federal government prioritizes individual freedom and self-reliance over cradle-to-grave government reliance that can ultimately lead to groupthinking conformist drones.

Progressivism, on the other hand, wants everyone to have fish. Imagine Oprah working at Pike Place Market: *You get a fish! You get a fish! You get a fish!* Progressives just want things to be good and fair, thinking every law, policy, and social construct should bend to what is deemed "good" or "fair" by the likes of politicians such as Bernie Sanders, AOC, or Ilhan Omar, yet they express little concern over math, economics, or reality. To paraphrase Benjamin Franklin, "[Progressive plans], like fish, begin to smell after three days."

In the twenty-first century we're more and more interested in having our fish caught, packaged, and delivered frozen. It may sound nice, but don't take the bait. Wouldn't you rather eat wild-caught Alaskan salmon than freezer-burned fish sticks? Of course you would.

The movie *Wall-E* comes to mind. The story takes place in 2805, seven hundred years after the Buy N Large corporation had taken over the Earth's economy. (Wait a minute! When did Disney become the bad guy in its own movies?!) Humanity is forced to live in giant space cruisers—one of which is called the Axiom—where every single modern convenience is on demand.

Hungry? Lunch is delivered in giant Slurpee-like cups. Bored?

Play simulated golf, shop online, or talk to virtual friends as you zoom around an advertiser's paradise. Don't know what to wear? That's okay. There are uniforms in your choice of red or blue. Fall out of your chair? Worry not! A service bot will be there to help you. What about babies? They hover in floating highchairs as they're brainwashed by robot teachers: *A is for Axiom, your home sweet home. B is for Buy N Large, your very best friend.*

When everything was handed to them, humanity had devolved into uniformed, boneless, consumerist blobs, lounging around in high-speed floating chairs. Sure, comfort and convenience was to be had at the touch of a button, but no one was truly happy or fulfilled. Everyone was surviving and everything was fair, but that just meant that no one was flourishing. What's worse, being that dependent made the people vulnerable to control. They no longer knew how to function without the machines, so the machines could control what they could see, do, or know. (Oh, and in case you're wondering, as of 2020, you can now buy the hover chairs from Segway.)[11]

The moment you become overly dependent or reliant on anything outside of yourself, it threatens your humanity. Whether it's Big Government programs, regulations, subsidies, Big Tech, or giant superstore corporations, when we wholly rely on things outside of ourselves, we give up freedom, opportunity, and personal accountability. Which is why the world depicted in *Wall-E* doesn't seem too far off. Besides the inevitable robot takeover, we've become more and more accustomed to dependence. We're reliant on institutions as our first line of defense against not only serious trouble but also the common realities of ordinary life: food and potable water, transportation, waste, mail. Of course, I'm not saying that these things aren't helpful, and some things like road construction or trash pickup should be covered by tax dollars, but it's important to think about all the aspects of our lives that are reliant on things outside of ourselves.

What saved the human blobs in *Wall-E* was their waking up to the power within their own selves. We see this play out through the character of Captain B. McCrea while he is under the control of AUTO, a steering-wheel-shaped robot *á la* HAL 9000 in *2001: A Space Odyssey* that functions as the ship's autopilot. Because the captain is so overweight, AUTO runs most of the ship's functions, but is secretly charged with the order of never returning to Earth.

The thing that wakes the captain up is the same thing that wakes us all up: the hope for something better. Suddenly, McCrea understood that he was meant for more than just sitting around being controlled; he could be an autonomous, free-thinking, and self-reliant human instead. Self-reliance eventually saves all of humanity living in 2805 and it can save us too right now. (Now, the only remaining question is if it will save us from the evil Disney corporation?!)

Mental Prepper

People may want you to think that God helps those who help others, but trust me: God helps those who help themselves.

At least that's what my grandma Mimi always said. When she was in her later years and was diagnosed with diabetes, cancer, and nearly every disease known to man, she still showed up to every family gathering, always helping out in the kitchen or buzzing around tidying up. I remember one time in particular, she was sitting on my parent's couch. It was a really, *really* cushy couch, so more than sitting on it, she was sitting *in* it. Her small frame looked trapped, almost as if the sofa were a torture device, and as she tried to get up, she struggled like she was climbing out of quicksand. Naturally, I rushed over to help, but she pushed me away saying, "No, David! God helps those who help themselves!"

I was thirty, and thought, *Uh, no, you got it wrong, Mimi. It's the opposite.* But as she continued to hoist herself up, moving a nearby table with her leg and using every single accent pillow for extra support, I realized that she was keeping her body as strong as she could despite being in physical decline. She was maintaining a sense of her own personal independence—physically, but more important, mentally. (Full transparency: I did at the final second give her one little push, but we'll just call that the helping hand of God.)

Throughout the past few decades, dozens of studies have shown that older people with a sense of self-reliance are more likely to live longer than older people without it. My grandma's physical health was in decline, sure, but she carried with her a spirit of self-reliance and mental readiness that not only kept her living longer but also inspired a sense of independence in her grandkids. I'm the living proof.

Physical preparedness and self-reliance is important, but it's nothing if you are not mentally fit. And if you're in a position of leadership, it's critical. Thank God we've got Joe Biden, right? Joking aside, the people that are in charge of us right now are in their seventies, eighties, and closing in on their nineties. As I write this now, Joe Biden is 78, Donald Trump is 75, Mitch McConnell is 79, Nancy Pelosi is in her seventh life as a vampire, and Senator Diane Feinstein is older than the Crypt Keeper. Sorry, more jokes!

This isn't to rail on America's golden girls and boys. There are nonagenarians that are more mentally and physically fit than people half their age. I, for one, would take Betty White over AOC any day. It's that we all have a duty to ensure that the work we're doing now is the work we're meant to be doing in *this* moment—and that we're doing it to the best of our ability. Sometimes we're physically and mentally up to snuff to actively lead (and this can be at any age!), but sometimes we're meant to inspire others with our spirit. I see you, Grammy!

When I think of mental readiness, Rudy Giuliani comes to mind. Say what you will about ol' Rudy today, with his hair dye running down his cheek (just let it go gray, Rudy), but there was a time that he was not only fit to lead, he was a great leader inspiring others to be great.

On September 11, 2001, I was living on the Upper East Side of Manhattan. I will never forget receiving a call from my dad as he watched the World Trade Center's South Tower crumble outside his office window.

That day changed New York City, and America, forever. It also happened to be the mayoral primary election day for NYC. As the mayor in his second, final term, Rudy woke up early, made coffee, had some breakfast, and expected to have a busy day at work. He was not expecting for his fair city to experience the most deadly terrorist attack in human history. Yet he stepped up to the plate and became a man whose steady and profound response to America's greatest tragedy transcended politics and transformed him into a national hero.

Rudy and I chatted on *The Rubin Report* in June 2020, and it became clear as he laid out his life story that mental readiness doesn't just arrive suddenly when it's needed. His personal mental readiness was created and fostered over the years leading up to 9/11—years spent fighting organized crime as district attorney, prosecuting over eight hundred members of the Mafia, and cleaning up the crime-ridden streets of Manhattan. In his words, "[Before 9/11] I'd been the mayor of New York [where] it's a crisis a week, an emergency a month, and a catastrophic emergency every six months. I mean, we had hurricanes, we had airplane crashes, we had subway derailments, we had hostage situations, we had terrorist attacks."

These experiences mentally prepared him to handle the worst crises imaginable. Day after day following the attack, he calmly explained the inexplicable, and reassured a traumatized city. I remember watching him every night on the evening news, as he walked amid the ash and rubble, thinking, *Thank God we have a leader like Rudy.* Every day, he was down at ground zero. The firefighters believed in him, the police believed in him, the public believed in him. He comforted survivors, he attended funerals, he urged residents to go back to living their lives and welcomed tourists, all the while exuding compassion and control over the situation.

Rudy Giuliani's greatness as New York City's mayor didn't come down to politics—it came down to a lifetime of real-world experience, preparing him for a moment to step up. In that moment he was a great leader not through some law, regulation, or new government program, but through the transformation of one life at a time through inspiring individuals to be great leaders themselves.

Bob Kerrey, a former Democratic governor and senator, a Vietnam veteran, and a member of the commission that studied 9/11, put it like this: "Trust me, the range of possibilities for leaders is quite extreme: Some panic, some get paralyzed. Giuliani was brave and reassuring, and you can't subtract that from his résumé."[12]

The recipe for great leadership is fairly simple but often takes a boatload of prior experiences to acquire: preparedness, tenacity, boldness, and self-reliance (and probably a dash of crazy). These ingredients are found within almost every great leader and allow the person to rise to the occasion and transcend the norm—from Rudy during 9/11 to FDR in the Great Depression and Churchill in WWII. Were these men human? Obviously. Were they also transcendent leaders? Inarguably.

But turns out, it's that very humanity that makes for great leadership as well. In a 2001 article published days after 9/11, a quote stands out from a seventy-three-year-old retired jewelry merchant and registered Democrat, Irving Perline: "The very qualities that have caused so many flaps and feuds—Giuliani's chin-out pugnaciousness, his reluctance to compromise, his tendency to take things very personally—have proved to be exactly what a stricken city needs in its worst crisis."[13] Leadership and readiness is not a one-size-fits-all capability. It's taking your individual abilities and aptitudes and using them for a greater good. It's living your life well and not shying away from experiences that can help shape you to be wiser, stronger, and better equipped. And most of the time, it's merely rising to the occasion when no one else will or can.

Disaster can strike at any moment. From worldwide pandemics, terrorist attacks, riots, and weather emergencies to the smaller-scale catastrophes of flat tires and raided grocery stores, being physically and mentally prepared is critical (and often go hand in hand). Do you want to be the one who panics? Who becomes paralyzed and freezes under pressure? Or do you want to be the one who's prepared, reliable, and brings a sense of calm when it's needed most?

You never know when you may need to step up to the plate in a time of crises. Keep your wits sharp and your body fine-tuned. Be reliant on yourself so you can be a dependable leader for others.

Worst-case scenario? You put up a good fight when all hell breaks loose (or at minimum when you need to climb out of a marshmallow couch). Best-case scenario? When it comes to those luxurious times when there are no crises (should we ever see those days again) those same ideals will typically result in living both a longer life and a more meaningful one.

7

CAPITALISM > SOCIALISM

Don't stay in bed, unless you can make money
in bed.

George Burns

Moving Out, Moving Up

My family was once rooted in New York. Since the turn of the twentieth century—when one set of great-grandparents moved to the
Lower East Side from Belarus and the other from Lithuania to
Brooklyn—the family has grown and scattered all throughout the
city and its boroughs, eating our bagels and schmear, yelling at taxi-
cabs, and hating the G Train.

Alas, as of now, the once multitudinous New York Rubins are
nearing extinction. Only two family members remain—one in Manhattan and one in Brooklyn. With rising taxes, higher cost of living, growing crime, and a power-hungry government, they've slowly
trickled out over the years. As of this writing, shootings are up 77
percent from last year. The Big Apple is nothing like it used to be:
in May 2021, a four-year-old was wounded by stray bullets on a

Saturday afternoon in Times Square.[1] We'll see how long the last of the Rubins stay put.

My sister was the most recent to leave. She had planned to live in New York City with her husband and two kids until the day she died. She lived in a forty-floor high-rise on the Upper West Side and paid $5,000 a month for a converted one bedroom, inventively slicing the living room into two rooms creating a windowless (and admittedly depressing) living space. She called it "my little shoe box." In 2020 she jumped ship, first moving to the suburbs, and then ultimately deciding to move to freedom-lovin' Florida. I guess when you're forced to spend 24/7 trapped inside your home, you realize the importance of having a home you actually like.

But the idiotic price per square foot, insanely high taxes, and escalating rate of crime (in fact, 2020 saw New York's bloodiest year in a decade—thanks, de Blasio) was only half the problem. Literally.

Half of her building was rent-controlled, so while some, like my sister, paid $5,000 for her little shoe box, others paid a mere $400 for the exact same apartment. Take it from a former New Yorker: to hear that a friend managed to land a rent-controlled apartment in some desirable neighborhood was the equivalent of Charlie getting the golden ticket and inheriting the whole damn factory while you're getting juiced in the Juicing Room after a bad chewing-gum trip. Oompa loompa doompadee duped.

To keep the rent-controlled apartments in the family, several generations would live under one roof—grandparents, parents, and grandchildren. Through rent control, government welfare checks, and food stamps, they managed to have the same housing for little to no personal responsibility. And who could blame them? For four hundred bucks a month, they could live in a nice neighborhood, in a nice building with a doorman. To leave Manhattan would mean to work their asses off, move to an outer borough, and commute an hour or more to get into the city.

So along with the apartment was an inheritance mindset as well, keeping these people in cycles of welfare and poverty rather than forcing them to be creative and resourceful.

This mindset keeps them in survival mode. Food? Check. Roof over head? Check. But does very little in promoting a thriving life that we're all capable of.

But, Dave, things like rent control, welfare, higher minimum wage, and food stamps help poor people and particularly marginalized people of color!

I used to think that too. In fact, my old lefty days were wholly defined by that line of thinking. I mean, what kind of cold-hearted monster wouldn't want to help the poor?

But over time, I came around to a hard but undeniable truth: the progressive welfare state does nothing to help people and it ruins our greatest cities because of it. Enforcement of quality-of-life violations is decreased, public space is given to the homeless and the drug addicts, and welfare checks are pumped out that promote dependency over responsibility. What does this do? Increase the rates of crime, homelessness, and poverty. It's a sick but logical irony. So, once-beloved cities like San Francisco, Seattle, Portland, and New York are taking the hit, leaving many taxpaying, middle-class residents disillusioned, leading to historical exoduses not seen since Moses. Let my people go . . . and not get shanked on the subway as they leave.

In reality (a place that progressives rarely visit), opposition to welfare and specifically rent control spans the political spectrum. Swedish socialist economist Assar Lindbeck famously said, "In many cases rent control appears to be the most efficient technique presently known to destroy a city—except for bombing it."[2] That's a *Swedish socialist* at that, so you know it must be bad.

But, hey, don't take it from me. I grew up in a middle-class family, riding bikes on Long Island.

Take it from a poor, orphan New Yorker (who happens to be black—if that kind of thing matters to you).

Sowell Searching

As far as public intellectuals go, few have been more prolific than economist Thomas Sowell. The man has written about a book a year since 1971, in addition to writing syndicated columns and academic articles *plus* teaching courses at Cornell, UCLA, Amherst, Brandeis, and Stanford. Needless to say, he's kept pretty busy.

Sowell was born in 1930 into a house with no electricity nor central heating or running water, and little to no food. His father died before he was born and his mother, a maid, died a few years later. He was adopted by his great-aunt and raised by her two daughters: three uneducated women who called him "Young Tommy." When he was eight years old, they moved from Gastonia, North Carolina, to Harlem, New York City, which opened up doors when it came to receiving a better education. Sowell worked his way through the elite, highly selective Stuyvesant High School (which, predictably, is crumbling under diversity and inclusions quotas these days) but dropped out at the age of seventeen due to financial hardships. He worked several jobs to support himself, including at a machine shop and as a messenger for Western Union delivering telegrams.

In his early twenties, Sowell considered himself a Marxist, finding it the best solution when it came to grappling with the immense housing inequality that he saw across the neighborhoods of New York City. In 1951, he was drafted into the Korean War and was assigned to the US Marine Corps, in the photography unit, where he would pick up the longtime hobby of photography. After Sowell was discharged, he enrolled at Howard University and eventually transferred to Harvard to graduate magna cum laude with a Bachelor of Arts degree in economics. In 1959, he earned a Master of Arts in economics from Columbia University and, in 1968, a PhD in economics from the University of Chicago. Despite being taught by some of the greatest thinkers of free-market capitalism, like George Stigler and Milton Friedman, he still thought Marxism was the most practical market system.

Soon after graduating with his fancy PhD, Sowell landed a summer internship at the US Department of Labor. Finally he could start really helping people. At last, theory could become practice.

Or so he thought.

Sowell's biggest concern at the time was minimum wages. After diving deep and immersing himself in the data, he found that minimum-wage hikes cause people who are unskilled to lose jobs completely. Eager to share those findings, he presented his research to the higher-ups with some practical next steps. Expecting an enthusiastic, *Congrats! You've done it!* the government workers instead sat there in silence and looked at one another stunned with expressions that read: *This idiot is going to ruin us all.*

It was in that moment Sowell realized that the US Department of Labor had its own agenda. The government didn't give a crap about whether or not it worked or didn't work—helped or didn't help. It had little interest in balancing inequality or in helping the marginalized, and a much bigger interest in keeping the poor dependent on the government.

It was that realization that turned Sowell's life around.

In 2018, I had arguably the best moment of my entire career when I sat down with him at Stanford University for an interview. I asked him, "You were a Marxist at one time in your life—what was your wake-up to what was wrong with that line of thinking?"

"Facts."

As he dove into research that one summer interning at the US Department of Labor, Sowell realized that a higher minimum wage doesn't necessarily translate into a better quality of life for all, but rather higher unemployment. In his words:

> The history of black workers in the United States illustrates the point. From the late nineteenth century on through the middle of the twentieth century, the labor force participation rate of American blacks was slightly higher than that of American whites. In other words, blacks were just as employable at the wages they received as whites were at their very different wages. The minimum wage law changed that. Before federal minimum wage laws were instituted in the 1930s, the black unemployment rate was slightly *lower* than the white unemployment rate in 1930. But then followed the Davis-Bacon Act of 1931, the National Industrial Recovery Act (NIRA) of 1933 and the Fair Labor Standards Act (FLSA) of 1938—all of which imposed government-mandated minimum wages, either on a particular sector or more broadly . . .

By 1954, black unemployment rates were double those
of whites and have continued to be at that level or higher.
Those particularly hard hit by the resulting unemployment have been black teenage males.[3]

What does this mean? It means that although minimum wage
sounds good, the facts explain why the most vulnerable workers are
the group that is *most* harmed by progressive minimum-wage laws.
Intentions can be good while the actual consequences can be catastrophic. And so it goes, the once-leftist Sowell was a Marxist no longer. The lofty visions of a rainbow, unicorn, butterfly utopia that
often fill the heads of progressives came face-to-face with reality and
hard facts. In Sowell's words: "The vision of the left—and I think
many conservatives underestimate this—is really a more attractive
vision in itself. The only reason for not believing it is that it doesn't
work. But you don't see that at the outset if all you're looking at is
theory. If the world were the way the left conceives it to be it would be
a better world than the way the right conceives it to be. It just happens that the world is not that way."[4]

Man, he's good.

But look, I get it. Healthcare for all, free college, cheap rent, higher
minimum wages, and food stamps all sound great and meaningful
and good. But how is it really helping? Better yet, *who* is it really
helping?

The Left promotes resentment and oppression and makes loud demands for "rights" to what other people have earned and produced.
One of the most sick, twisted things Bernie Sanders did was make
greed a lofty goal—he somehow made the idea of being *entitled* to
what someone has be a worthy, moral pursuit. Lots of ideas, little

progress, doing next to nothing for the poor other than make them more unhappy. However, what it *does* do is lift the Left to positions of power and self-aggrandizement, giving them airtime to promote socially counterproductive (read: damaging) policies. It's like all they want is power or something?! Sowell puts it like this: "Although the big word on the left is 'compassion,' the big agenda on the left is dependency. The more people are dependent on government handouts, the more votes the left can depend on for an ever-expanding welfare state."[5]

Which is why Sowell's main message can be boiled down to this: the reason some people are poor is not discrimination, exploitation, or corruption on the part of the rich, but rather, people are poor because they don't or *won't* produce (and often the government keeps them from stepping up to the plate to do so). As Sowell writes:

> You cannot take any people, of any color, and exempt them from the requirements of civilization—including work, behavioral standards, personal responsibility and all the other basic things that the clever intelligentsia disdain—without ruinous consequences to them and to society at large.
>
> Non-judgmental subsidies of counterproductive lifestyles are treating people as if they were livestock, to be fed and tended by others in a welfare state—and yet expecting them to develop as human beings have developed when facing the challenges of life themselves.[6]

Time and time again, the data shows that by providing handouts, you force people into complacency and dependency on a system that does not care about them or their unique set of circumstances. No work and government pay makes Jack a dull boy. In fact, Census Bureau data reveals that the poverty rate was steadily falling in the 1950s and early 1960s, but then stagnated once the government intervened and the War on Poverty began. Since then, U.S. taxpayers have spent over $22 trillion on anti-poverty programs.[7]

Okay, hold up.

Did you see that? That's 22 trillion buckaroos. That's nearly *80 percent* of our current national debt. When you live in a country whose own debt could put us on the brink of global warfare, that is a ridiculous amount of money. And it's one thing if these programs would have actually worked and lifted people out of poverty, but the progress toward alleviating poverty has been minimal, if not completely backward.

Well, that's *almost* true. In 2019, the poverty rate for the United States was 10.5 percent, the lowest since estimates were first released for 1959, five years before the government intervened in 1964 with its War on Poverty. In fact, in 2018 and 2019 poverty rates declined 18.8 percent and 15.7 percent, respectively, for black and Hispanic origin groups.[8]

Not only did the poverty rate for black origin groups fall to all-time record lows in 2019, but it also fell below 20 percent for the first time since 1959, the year poverty estimates were first released for this group.[9] Plus, that year more black households earned six-figure incomes than the year before.[10] In fact, the only thing disrupting the decline was job loss that came with strict quarantine guidelines in 2020.

Additionally, the rate of new entrepreneurs from 2016 to 2019 surged, particularly in women-owned businesses, averaging eighteen thousand new businesses a day. Firms owned by women of color grew at double the rate of that for all women.[11]

Okay, well this doesn't make any sense. The racist, orange, capitalist pig was in office! During that time, the villainous Trump was ruthlessly making massive cuts to health, housing, and other low-income assistance programs. No way that progrowth policies like reducing the government's welfare spending and empowering people through less regulation, corporate tax cuts, and implementing reforms that bolster work expectations to be able to receive entitlements like food stamps could *actually* work. Are we really saying here that promoting individual freedom and personal responsibility *benefits* the most marginalized and poor? You'd have to be a racist bigot to believe all that!

Despite all this incredibly good news—higher employment rates and higher salaries for people of color and more business opportunities for women of color—the Left wasn't happy. During the 2020 State of the Union address, Trump stated, "We are advancing with unbridled optimism and lifting our citizens of every race, color, religion and creed very, very high." Yet, progressives became AOC (Apoplectic on Cue) and decided not to attend in protest, and Nancy Pelosi, the hated self-righteous neighbor out of a *Golden Girls* episode, tore up the printed speech at its closing. And who could forget the image of all the Democrat women wearing "suffragette white" during the 2019 State of the Union, crossing their arms as he talked about the progress made.

Young Tommy Sowell could spot what was going on: Democrats didn't care about helping the poor; they cared about increasing their power at the poor's expense.

Numbers don't lie, and yet the outcome of the 2020 presidential election made one thing clear: in contemporary America, facts don't win . . . feelings do.

The future for America—for all of us: the tired, the poor, the huddled masses yearning to breathe free—is dependent on a prioritization of independence over dependency, of personal responsibility over handouts, and of facts over feelings. Because facts don't care about your feelings. (Shapiro, I owe you five bucks!)

Sowell said it best. "Please take to heart the lesson of what happens when you vote on the basis of rhetoric and symbolism instead of using your mind. It doesn't matter how smart you are unless you think."[12]

Yeah, this guy's *really* good.

The Facts or Feelings Economy

When it comes to facts and reality, conservatives have a better grasp than virtually any other group.

We know, for instance, that "Medicare for all" means bloating the federal budget and sinking further into a bottomless pit of national debt and despair. Plus, requiring doctors and medical entrepreneurs to only use government policies would mean no more medical advancements toward lowering costs and lengthening life span (and say bye-bye to the dream of someday curing cancer!).

We know that the $15-per-hour wage floor hurts small businesses and causes the most at-risk to lose jobs, eventually replacing humans with glorified iPads. Between higher wages and the inevitable push for technology over people, mom-and-pop shops would be forced to close, which means, yet again, less opportunity, less innovation, and less human spirit. (I mean, where does the cheesecake taste better, at The Cheesecake Factory or at your local cake shop? Ya know, the one that was forced to close its doors forever over COVID regulations...)

We know that high tax rates hurt economic growth and entrepreneurial spirit. This one's so obvious it's stupid that we're all still talking about it. If someone starts a business by doing something they love—opening a restaurant or selling tie-dye shirts on Etsy—the less money going toward taxes means more money going into the business and toward employing staff (and even possibly paying them *more* than $15 dollars an hour).

Yeah, facts and reality are *not* typically a problem for conservatives.

But there is a downside to focusing exclusively on facts. This tendency has distracted us from making strong ethical arguments that speak to the emotional reality of people's lives. It's not that once-idealistic youths like Sowell and me—and bleeding-heart twenty-first century wokesters—are bad people—it's that they got duped by all the progressive-leftist propaganda that left them feeling sad, angry, happy, or resentful. (I mean is anyone *really* disputing the notion that black lives matter?) When we say that nothing matters besides the financial and economic data, we inadvertently risk ceding the culture war.

For a long time, the Left's reputation was mostly one of being nice, good, compassionate people, while conservatives were often considered greedy, compassionless capitalists. The irony? Studies have consistently shown that when putting their money where their mouths are, conservatives donate a much larger amount of cash to causes they care about than their lefty counterparts. If you're thinking that this is because they're richer, you'd be wrong. Conservatives donate a higher percentage of their incomes (which, interestingly enough, were slightly lower than that of liberals).[13]

Dammit! There I go again with friggin' facts! By only using facts and not making the very true, ethical case that concepts like individualism and capitalism are stronger tools for helping even the most marginalized, we allow progressives to assume that they own the market on goodness.

This is why the culture wars matter. It's more than fighting about Dr. Seuss books being banned for being racist (they weren't) or forcing Mr. Potato Head to come out as nonbinary. (I guess, to be fair, I am not sure how he/she/they/ze identifies.) Sure, these decisions have huge ethical implications, but as products they have economic consequences as well. Which is why the culture wars focus on two competing visions for America's future: capitalist or socialist. Capitalism means that there are voluntary trades for mutual self-interest and mutual benefit, creating scenarios within which everyone can win. Socialism is compulsory, forcing people to play a game where if one side is winning, the other is losing. If one climbs the ranks, another is being oppressed. Capitalism unites people under the idea that everyone can participate; socialism divides them into winners and losers.

Capitalism has long been thought of as an everyone-for-themselves-do-whatever-you-want-get-as-much-as-you-can-steal-and-cheat-to-get-to-the-top ideology, but that couldn't be more wrong.

In 2019 I sat down with John A. Allison, the former president and CEO of the Cato Institute, the leading think tank for libertarian thought. We chatted a lot about the above, but also discussed his personal story of being the longest-serving CEO of a top-25 financial institution, Branch Banking and Trust, or BB&T.

Allison is a prime example of what ethics and capitalism look like in practice. It all began when he stumbled upon Ayn Rand in college, captivated by her essay collection *Capitalism: The Unknown Ideal.* He didn't just become an Ayn Rand fan—he became a devotee, subscribing to her philosophies of capitalism and individualism and practicing them throughout his entire life and career. According to Rand, capitalism is a social system that recognizes individual rights (including the right to property), while limiting government intervention in the economy. At all. Laissez-faire capitalism is capitalism in its purest form, meaning, literally, "let us be." With capitalism, the individual can flourish. In fact, it's the only system that recognizes man as a rational, autonomous being who "has the *right* to exist for his own sake" free from coercion by institutions or by others.[14]

Objectivism is at the heart of capitalism, Rand states: "[T]he concept of man as a heroic being, with his own happiness as the moral purpose of his life, with productive achievement as his noblest activity, and reason as his only absolute."[15] In other words, if each individual pursues his or her own personal happiness at all costs, the world would become a better place for everyone.[16]

Remember, this individualist, capitalist, modern-conservative stuff is all about the *pursuit of happiness*. It's that very fine line between surviving (government dependency, welfare, and food stamps) and thriving (personal responsibility, entrepreneurship, and hard work).

Of course, there are greedy dog-eat-dog businessmen who ruthlessly walk over people to get to the top. They've got their yachts and their nice houses now, but living a life solely at the expense of others has its consequences. My hunch is those people aren't all that happy either. In my experience, those folks are usually the most nihilistic, burnt out, and depressed. Plus, you can only get away with this self-indulgent behavior for so long. Remember that Bernie Madoff guy?

Not John Allison. With individualism as his true-north philosophy, he joined BB&T at twenty-three years old in 1971, becoming CEO when he was forty. As he climbed the ranks, he started instilling more and more individualist values and virtues within his company's culture, assigning Rand's *Atlas Shrugged* to all of his senior executives, calling it "the best defense of capitalism ever written."[17]

Then came the "Great Recession."

In a nutshell, the 2008 stock market crash came down to two things: the government sticking its nose where it shouldn't and people taking on loans they couldn't afford. Many banks loosened their strict lending standards to award credit to people who couldn't otherwise qualify, driving up the housing prices that they couldn't otherwise afford. The banks made tons of short-term cash, providing subprime mortgage loans left and right until the market crashed.

While other banks experienced record-breaking losses, BB&T didn't record a single quarterly loss—not because its staff were strategic geniuses but because with capitalism and individualism at its core, they remained wildly ethical and therefore extremely successful. Everything they did was to help the client be set for financial success by not giving them subprime loans that they wouldn't be able to afford in the long-term. In doing so, it set the bank up for success as well. Just capitalist self-interest doing its thing.

But beyond ethics, Allison didn't engage in subprime lending because he recognized early on that subprime loans were a dangerous product of a system distorted by Federal Reserve regulations. He goes in depth in his book, *The Financial Crisis and the Free Market Cure*, but I'll provide a little bit of his 2008 Recession 101 here.

Think of it like this: The US Federal Reserve bank is kind of like the central bank for America. In trying to avoid a natural market correction that was happening in the early 2000s, it printed a bunch of extra money. This laid the soapy foundation for the housing bubble by keeping interest rates artificially low, making borrowing super affordable. In fact, for a while, interest rates were lower than the rise in prices, so people basically got paid to borrow money.[18] Who could blame them for cashing in?

Government-sponsored enterprises Fannie Mae and Freddie Mac stepped in and guaranteed loans for as many Americans as possible, including people with little or no credit. What happened? These GSEs created a new and growing market for these so-called subprime loans (the type of loans John Allison and BB&T wouldn't give).

Naturally, millions of Americans got in on the action. Everyone started to go after homes, creating a bidding war. But what does this do? Increase the demand for housing as well as the prices. Thus, the housing bubble was blown.

But it didn't take long to pop. The Federal Reserve then raised the interest rates from 2004 to 2006 because of fears that it had printed *too* much money. Imagine that. Suddenly, those who had been thinking about buying a house gave up on the idea, because now they couldn't afford the loan. Those who could afford their mortgage for a while couldn't anymore and were forced to sell their homes. With that, housing demand fell and so did housing prices. *Pop!* The US economy tanked, destroying trillions of dollars of wealth and mil-lions of jobs.[19]

And how did the government respond when the too-big-to-fail in-stitutions started failing? It made those institutions bigger, slapping Band-Aids onto carotid arteries that they themselves had opened.

Yet anti-capitalists blamed it on a lack of regulations and govern-ment oversight.

The irony? The Great Recession is exactly what it looks like when there is *no* free-market capitalism. Something like this could never happen under laissez-faire capitalism. Instead, the failing compa-nies would be left alone to fail—paying the consequences for their unethical business dealings, while decent, ethical companies would remain to rise to the top.

Capitalism isn't the problem. The only thing it didn't do well is make a good defense for itself. Daddy government and its constant meddling is the problem . . . again. (Are you starting to get it yet?! The government isn't your daddy!)

A truly healthy society would have said, "Hey, banks, you effed up, and now you're going to have to die." But instead, we saved them and what followed was tragic. The government bailed out large insti-tutions that should have been allowed to tank at the expense of mom-and-pop businesses. Allison saw this firsthand as he worked with a lot of small construction companies—business owners that had only a couple of trucks, for example, and three employees. The system al-lowed them to fail while the big guys got saved. The worst part? Large companies that didn't even need saving were forced to take the gov-ernment dole. In fact, leadership at healthy banks like BB&T felt compelled to accept some bailout money to obscure the fact that the government was simply trying to save the big banks. What happens? The national debt gets bigger and only the little guy suffers.

Listen, people! Economic meltdowns aren't typically the effects of capitalism—capitalism seeks to create win-win scenarios. The problem is socialist compulsion: using government force to decide the winners and losers.

But to be fair, there was another culprit, albeit one slightly more innocent. The reality of the crash was that financially, people bit off more than they could chew. It was heartbreaking—people losing their jobs and homes—but it doesn't take a financial expert to understand that a job paying forty-thousand dollars annually *prooobably* can't pay for a two-million-dollar mansion. It's like Monopoly, but real! Rarely do you move from Baltic Avenue to Park Place in one move. Instead, you have to save up, maybe even play a few rounds, but eventually you can move to Oriental Avenue. (Wait, can we still call it that?!)

In the period leading up to the bubble burst, most potential buyers seemed unwilling to live within their means, and thus the bank bailouts outsourced fiscal responsibilities to the machine, which really does not give two shits about anything other than keeping the machine nice and greasy.

You see, the hard thing about all this capitalist, free-market, conservative, individualist, freedom-lovin' stuff is that it points the finger at *you*. Personal responsibility means you own the choices you make. And although it's your choice to pursue the very things that make *you* happy, you accept the consequences of your decisions, whatever they may be.

It's Personal

In Rand's *Atlas Shrugged*, one of the heroes, Francisco d'Anconia, gives a speech about the meaning of money: "The words 'to make money' hold the essence of human morality." In what way, you ask? Well, think about how people make money. We make money through production and trade—things that spring from human ingenuity, creativity, and relationships. A productive, rational, independent thinker creates value and then gains value from others through voluntary exchange. Feels pretty noble and moral to me.

Yet people claim that money is the root of all evil. Folks, it just ain't true—money is not an end in itself. It's people's out-of-whack relationship with money that's evil, and their inability to take life seriously. Money's value only exists to the extent of what someone does with it—that is, money is nothing more than a tool for constructing the life you want.

Two people can have the exact same amount of money. One might really, really want to hoard it and not live an extravagant life to better be able to retire early, while the other might love going on lush vacations and drinking super expensive bottles of wine with friends. Carpe dime versus carpe diem. Neither one is necessarily better or worse, as long as you're doing the one that you want to be doing.

Which is why my personal philosophy around money is pretty simple: *Don't be a dumbass, live within your means, and do what you want with the money you've earned.*

For me, that looks like investing my money in physical things. Property, for example, feels tangible, plus with mortgage rates being so low these days, I don't mind paying my mortgage because it kind of feels like I'm paying myself. Every month, I feel happy to be able to make that payment and continue to enjoy my home. Each mortgage bill reminds me of the hard work it took to be able to pay for my home, and this fills me with a sense of pride and gratitude. (That's kinda the human morality bit that Rand's talking about.) Then, if and when the time comes, it's mine to sell or do with it what I will. Despite the real-estate market being a fluctuating one, it still seems more stable than nearly any other financial investment, slightly more dependent on the natural market than on the system itself (albeit not always, as we've learned). Even in the worst-case scenario, I have a place to lay my head at the end of each day.

As all our institutions crumble around us, financial instruments like 401(k)s and Roth IRAs sound like vestiges of the Old World. Sure, I have some money in both of those accounts, but can we really trust them to be there when we need them? Of course, I'm in no way saying that you should not plan for retirement, but one would be wise to question antiquated financial advice. Even a healthy consideration of things like cryptocurrency and silver could make or break your financial future. But it's quite possible that being creative with your investments or starting a risky business now could pay off more than saving 2 to 6 percent of your earned monthly income toward something you may or may not ever benefit from in the future.

At the end of the day, you don't have to be a financial genius or obsessed with money or markets to do it right and live your life well. You just have to take personal responsibility for it and really *think* about and plan for what makes you happy. Do you really need *more* shirts? Did that last unnecessary purchase really make you feel any happier? Maybe it did—and that's great!—but maybe it didn't. Instead, opt for taking care of your future goals and the people you care about within your orbit. Reflect carefully on your spouse's needs, your children's needs, and your community's needs. Because the only way we can get out of this philosophical, economic culture war we're fighting is to step up and do the damn thing: Condemn welfare through personal altruism. Denounce socialism's hypocrisy by embodying capitalism's values and ethics. Create a healthier parallel economy compared with the woke, self-destructing one. And be self-reliant, not reliant on a system that cares more about power than your happiness.

The shape our lives form is up to us. Sure, some are born with more, some are born with less, but there are endless adventures possible to each of us. By recognizing what you can't control and taking responsibility for what you can, you really can create a rich life worth its weight in gold (or bitcoin).

8

THE EIGHTEENTH-CENTURY LESBIAN POETRY TRAP

> Find a job you enjoy doing, and you will never
> have to work a day in your life.
>
> Mark Twain

Odd Jobs

It was 1999: the year Bill Clinton was acquitted, the euro was created, *SpongeBob SquarePants* premiered, Nintendo's Game Boy Color hit the shelves, and yours truly worked as the assistant manager for an Electronics Boutique in the illustrious Broadway Mall in Hicksville, Long Island.

I loved video games, and being a young, spry twenty-three-year-old, I went into that job thinking it was going to be the coolest thing ever. And frankly, for a few days, it was. That first week I enthusiastically inspected the newly delivered, fresh, plastic-wrapped games, mentally processing what my next buy would be once I racked up some cash. (Donkey Kong 64 or Super Smash Brothers? Maybe both—thank god for my 10 percent discount.) When my lunch break rolled around, I would head over to the food-court metropolis. Auntie Anne's, Sbarro, Taco Bell, Wok & Roll—the options were limitless. Talk about living the dream.

But it didn't take long for my nineties paradise to become a linoleum-enclosed and fluorescent-lit prison. Eleven pounds and a few too many pimples later, I realized that Mario and Zelda don't stop by to take you out for an Orange Julius and that the wafting smell of Abercrombie perfume really begins to grate on you after a couple days. By the time Christmas rolled around I was on the brink of throwing myself down the escalators. Every day—from Thanksgiving to New Year's—I heard the same looped Christmas music. Even now, if I ever hear Mariah Carey's "All I Want for Christmas Is You," it'll be too soon, and my PTSD flairs when I hear the very dangerous and highly misogynistic "Baby It's Cold Outside."

I already knew I didn't want to spend my life hocking Sonic the Hedgehog and Crash Bandicoot. I had a much more healthy goal in mind, of course. With my freshly printed diploma, showing *Bachelors in Political Science* stamped front and center, I was ready for a long, stable career as . . . a stand-up comedian. Which is why when I wasn't working at Electronics Boutique, I was an intern at *The Daily Show*. Having just graduated, I wasn't technically eligible for the internship, but not willing to give up on the opportunity, I forged a letter from Binghamton University. Jon Stewart had just taken over, so for three days a week I got to watch him do his thing, dreaming of the day I too could be the host of *The Tonight Show*, or better yet, my *own* show. Can you imagine?

In the evenings, I did stand-up at open-mic nights six nights a week, two gigs each night. I would hand out comedy tickets in Times Square in the rain, sleet, and snow. Those early years, I did everything I could to make some cash while still pursuing the dream of stand-up, including working catering gigs and writing jokes on the back of napkins to use for later shows, landscaping a brownstone on a Saturday afternoon and then rushing to The Comedy Cellar at night, handing out tchotchkes for some promotional company at an event, and chatting up people who had ins at different clubs.

Eventually, when the new millennium rolled around and Y2K didn't kill us all, I left my internship at *The Daily Show* (and my fancy job at Electronics Boutique) to devote myself full-time to the comedy-club hustle. I was twenty-four but I was already burnt out—just young enough to be frustrated with how young I was and just old enough to be sick of the racket.

One November morning I had woken up on a couch in New Jersey after a late-night gig. I hopped on a train into New York City and met a friend at the Starbucks in Rockefeller Center. We had met at The Comedy Cellar a few months back and had both been complaining about the scene for a few months—late nights for little pay just didn't seem all that worth it. So, we had come up with an idea: an original live-audience television show. Cool! Great idea! Only problem was that none of us were rich or born into families with media connections, and we were broke comics with no money for rent, let alone disposable income for studio rental space.

My friends had jobs as NBC pages, making ten bucks an hour to take Peacock-clad tourists behind the scenes of shows like *Saturday Night Live*, *The Today Show*, or *The Tonight Show with Conan O'Brien*. Think Kenneth Parcell from *30 Rock*. But there was one lesser known stop on the tour: a miniature news studio on the ninth floor, right above Studio 8H, the home of *SNL*. It wasn't a working studio, but instead a kind of play-set where tourists could sit behind a news desk or stand in front of a weather map and pose for the camera. That afternoon after coffee, my friend showed me this secret, oft-forgotten spot. Our show scouting consisted of only this location, and it was perfect. The only thing was that NBC would never allow us to use the studio, so we just decided to never ask anybody and just do it ourselves. We went rogue. Technically that was my idea as I was the only one who didn't work at NBC, so I personally had nothing to lose.

Seven months of rehearsals, saving money, and many technical difficulties later, we were ready for our premiere. On March 24, 2001, we began secretly filming our own comedy show, *The Anti-Show* in the NBC Studios of the legendary Rockefeller Plaza. It was *The Daily Show* meets *SNL*'s "Weekend Update," and for about eighty bucks an episode, we created a live show with a script, a producer, a crew of cameramen, a makeup artist, cue-card holders, and a guy to warm up the live, in-studio audience.

With about forty people in the seats, I opened with, "What you are about to see is probably the most groundbreaking show in the history of television. We are at an unused studio at one of the Big Three networks here in New York City. Nobody from the network knows that we're here—if they did, we'd probably spend the rest of the night in jail."

I paused dramatically.

"With that in mind, welcome to *The Anti-Show*."

For about a year, we ran the whole thing on local public-access television. With each show performed, it became more refined and polished, and by the end, we had proved that if you really wanted something you could figure out another way to do it—with or without permission.

But it all didn't go exactly as planned. We had hopes of getting picked up by some bigwig network (back when I cared about that kind of thing), and it never really came together. But it paid in dividends. It taught me the lesson early on that the system is not very accommodating of dreams, and if you want to fight the system you have to do things differently. I was taught that same lesson repeatedly—jumping from gig to gig, network to network, only to eventually realize that to create the life I wanted I would have to do it myself.

You may be sensing a pattern in my life. Everything has come down to taking matters into my own hands. What I've realized is there is rarely some deep injustice that's aimed at you, making things difficult; most of the time it's just life being life.

You can't just sit and wait for the dream job or opportunity to fall into your lap. You can't expect the world to take care of you. You've got to step up to the plate (assuming there is even a plate to step up to—and if not, you make that damn plate, or maybe you don't even need a plate at all!). You've got to create opportunities, even when there aren't any.

When it comes to our work life, it doesn't all come together perfectly overnight. There are times when you're stocking shelves with the new Pokémon games, doing lawn work, catering gigs, and hustling 'til the sun comes out. Then there are times where work feels meaningful and time folds in on itself because the flow feels so rhythmic. (Fortunately and unfortunately, neither lasts forever). It may sound a bit hoity-toity, but the key to all of this is to have some sort of dream—some kind of North Star to shoot for beyond where you are in each moment.

And while I am not condoning forged college letters or breaking and entering into large corporations, there are always ways to be, *ahem*, "creative" when it comes to aligning the way you want to live your life and the way you make a living.

Actually, I am totally condoning those things. You gotta do what you gotta do.

On the Clock

Following the industrial revolution, it was common for people to work ten to sixteen hours a day for six days a week. Eventually, people started calling for an eight-hour workday, the common slogan of the movement being, "Eight hours for work, eight hours for rest, eight hours for what we will." By the early 1900s, many industries adopted the eight-hour workday, but most people were still working six days. That all changed when in 1926, Henry Ford removed one required day of work from his employee schedule, turning a six-day schedule into five days. Thus, the forty-hour workweek was born.

Ford didn't act from a place of charity or compassion, mind you; it was just capitalism doing what capitalism does best. He realized quickly that with reduced hours, workers were exponentially more productive. Ford's actions also created something called the freakin' *weekend*. More free time meant more people buying products. Better work conditions resulted in an overall better economy. In his words, "Leisure is an indispensable ingredient in a growing consumer market because working people need to have enough free time to find uses for consumer products, including automobiles."[1] Hear that, folks? You can also thank capitalism for Saturdays and Sundays.

Ford's successes caught on and resulted in manufacturing companies all over the world adopting a nine-to-five lifestyle and better working conditions. By the time President Roosevelt signed the Fair Labor Standards Act of 1938, mandating a forty-hour workweek, it was pretty much unnecessary. For decades leading up to the Act's passing, natural market forces had been driving down the average workweek.

For decades, despite evolving technology, work pretty much looked the same. Clock in at 9:00 a.m., clock out at 5:00 p.m.

Until now.

In March 2020, millions of people were thrown into a sudden experiment: *working from home*. What was supposed to be a two-week stint quickly turned into the "new normal." (Man, I just hate that phrase.)

As a work-from-home veteran, it was kind of funny watching news anchors and TV personalities scramble to create some kind of backdrop or strategically place a credibility bookshelf with all the right woke books in the Zoom camera's periphery. But take it from the guy who's run a show out of his garage—working from home has its perks. No arbitrary commute. No wasted time by the water cooler hearing about Shannon's bachelorette party. No bad office snacks. No fluorescent-lit atmosphere. No arbitrary schedule. No wasted time. Best of all, often no pants.

For too long, work functioned like the following: wake up begrudgingly, get into your car (or onto mass transportation), commute in rush-hour traffic, sit behind a desk for eight hours even when you don't necessarily need to, commute again, and arrive home depleted and uninspired . . . only to do the exact same thing the next day. For better or for worse, the pandemic forced the world into another

kind of industrial revolution, and if we can move past antiquated or-
thodoxy of suit-wearing, chained-to-your-desk work, there's an opportunity to free ourselves from complacency and inefficiency.

Think about all that wasted time. The average commute times for
Americans are 26.6 minutes a day, to and from work for a grand total
of 53.2 minutes of daily driving (or riding, if taking public transportation). Then there's the mandatory desk time—people are expected to just sit there, not because they're motivated and are
actually getting things done, but because it's not 5:00 p.m. yet. Oh,
and lest we forget the petty office drama with less-than-loved co-
workers. Admit it. You just don't like these people and there will
never be enough happy hours to fix that! Were we to combine all the
wasted seconds, minutes, and hours, you'd have the better part of
your day back.

Which is why, for many, work from home meant more *time*. Some
made the most of it, while some let the hours slip away gaining nothing but Postmates-induced pounds. Those that took advantage of the
situation had more time for family, more time for health, and more
time for working toward the life they wanted, whether that meant
personally or professionally. It's no coincidence that gardening and
raising backyard chickens have exploded in popularity since 2020
and many saw an increase of thirty more minutes of daily exercise.[2]
Ambitious and savvy dreamers finally had the time and space to
start their own side hustles and companies, kicking off what I hope
will be a new era of entrepreneurship in America.

And sure, while kitchen tables and recliners may not make the
best conference tables or desks, with the erosion of city centers as
the hub for places to work and huge office buildings sitting empty,
people can keep their big-city jobs and move to rural and suburban

areas. I'm telling you, New Yorkers, there is something called *a back-yard* and they make pretty good workspaces too. Plus, if small towns are willing to take in the coastal-city refugees, a thriving local economy and Main Street America renaissance could be in our future. (Just leave your lefty politics and at least *try* to understand what made these places more desirable.)

Either way, it seems like the new look of work was something that everyone could agree on. According to a 2020 study, only 12 percent wanted to return to full-time office work, and 72 percent wanted a hybrid remote-office model moving forward.[3] Even before the pandemic shut down offices, studies showed that full-time remote workers said they're happy at their job 22 percent more than people who never worked remotely.[4]

And it doesn't just benefit the employee. A 2020 study by Prodoscore reported an increase in work productivity by 47 percent since March 2020 compared with the previous year. Another survey showed that work-from-home employees spent 15 percent less time actively avoiding work and spent 1.4 more days working each month, despite taking more breaks.[5]

Wait a minute! This can't be true! Surely, more freedom and more liberty for more people can't always mean more progress and more productivity in all areas of life?

I'm kidding. It totally does.

For quite some time, companies have preferred top-down control, putting very little faith in their employees. To be fair, it makes sense to some degree. The ladder built into corporate structures demands that higher-ups ensure that lower-downs are hitting targets and doing what needs to be done. But it seems that some kind of workplace libertarianism or corporate individualism could lead to a much more thriving future—both for the individual and for companies large and small.

Imagine, prioritizing freedom over technocratic guidelines and empowering individuals to take more responsibility and accountability so that each feels more vested in the success of the company.

Turns out Ford wasn't the only automobile-based company that has paved the way for new ways to work.

Michelin, the international tire manufacturing company, with 114,000 employees, demonstrates what corporate freedoms and individualism looks like when rubber meets the road (see what I did there?). At one of its plants, teams self-direct their workday while operators set their own schedules, monitor their own performance, and are consulted on machinery upgrades. Since giving freedom to its employees, Michelin managed to nearly double its cash flow in only a couple of years from $1 billion in 2015 to $1.75 billion in 2017. In 2018, Michelin was ranked America's Best Large Employer.[6]

It's not rocket science, it's just individualism proving itself. People hate being micromanaged. Treating your employees as valuable, living, and breathing individuals with varying needs, rather than as some corporate collective, can go a pretty long way. Individualism offers freedom for employees to explore their own ways of completing their tasks without tyrannical control. By allowing people to take responsibility and accountability while making them feel vital to the company's success and not just a cog in the machine, you promote their general well-being. Keeping employees happy doesn't just mean the world is a better place (although that's great), it means they'll work harder for the company and put more money into everyone's pockets.

An individualist workplace emphasizes autonomy. Employees are praised and encouraged to take initiative and be self-starters, and the employer/employee relationship is based on mutual individual self-interest. Collectivism in the workplace, on the other hand, is just like plain ol' collectivism. It's a tool used to excuse those from taking responsibility, absolving people from any real sense of personal duty. Instead, responsibility and accountability is reduced to following orders, and work becomes a detested to-do list where nobody wins.

You see it a lot. People showing up to work and doing the bare minimum—accomplishing just enough to not get fired, but not enough to help the company grow, or more important, enable themselves to grow. These employees get stuck in jobs they hate, simply because they can coast under the radar without doing much. They become totally comfortable being in situations and adding no value at all, settling for complacency over contentment. Think about it for a moment—how much time do you spend on social media at work? Pretty sure that's not what they're paying you for!

Work doesn't have to look like that. Hell, *life* doesn't have to look like that.

When individuals feel empowered and free, they become more conscious of the life they lead—both in their personal and professional lives.

When I first struck out on my own and launched *The Rubin Report,* I was focused on creating a career that worked for me and my personal life. Over time, the business side of things has become more and more enjoyable for me. The minute I started employing people, I was forced to begin thinking about the type of company I want to run. It gave me an opportunity to really practice what I preach when it comes to participating in capitalism and individualism across all spheres.

So, when it comes to how I lead, I believe a few things are crucial.

First, I am a big believer in the idea that work should never be about hours; work should be about accomplishing things. I always tell my employees, I don't care when you do your work or how you do your work as long as I am not waiting on something when I am supposed to have it. If I think it's taking you six hours and you get it done in ten minutes, good for you. You can be a night owl or a morning person, just be on time.

Second, I believe work should also be understood by employers as just that: work. While I truly hope that all my employees feel fulfilled and a part of something bigger, I don't take that as an opportunity to not pay them well. So, I pay them very well, with annual raises and bonuses. All of them, interns included (unlike White House interns). Plus, I pay their health insurance and their dependents' insurance. All of it. I want them to enjoy their work and their lives so that when they arrive at the studio, they don't show up feeling resentful and unfulfilled, but appreciated and empowered.

Third, I try to keep the roads of communication open because when you're dealing with people, there is a mutual responsibility to communicate. If I am overloading an employee, but I don't know that I am overloading, it's that employee's responsibility to tell me.

Fourth, people excel at different things and often have different personalities. Creatives can be messy, and organized people can be controlling. So although we are currently a lean and tight-knit team, I try to let everybody do the work they're best at and actually enjoy. And when it comes to crap nobody wants to do, and there's always some of it, we at least try to evenly distribute it, myself included.

Last, call me a racist, homophobic bigot, but I hire based solely on skill and experience—not on race, gender, nor any other immutable characteristics. Groundbreaking, I know.

Sure, I like being a nice boss and want them to live good lives, but that's not the only reason I do it. It's in *my* self-interest to treat and pay my staff well and to include them as integral parts of the company we're building. The happier they are at work, the better my business grows. Likewise, I want it to be in *their* self-interest to work hard and be proactive. That's really what all this individualism stuff is about. Creating more thriving institutions, seeing yourself fully, and therefore seeing each person fully, wherever they may exist on the chain of command. When you treat people equally, promote personal growth, and encourage self-direction, you aren't just living out your individualistic beliefs, you are creating more successful companies, healthier employees, and a happier life of your own.

The old way of work is dead. "Eight hours for work, eight hours for rest, eight hours for what we will" just isn't the way we live anymore. In ways both good and bad, our lives and our livelihoods have merged together entirely. Our worlds can no longer be compartmentalized because the same technologies we use for work are the same ones we're using while at rest and when doing what we will.

By adapting to the times and adopting high-freedom policies, we can stop wasting time and choose contentment and commitment over complacency. We can envision new ways to live and work. With the crumbling of all our institutions and the bricks of corporate buildings strewn everywhere, there is an opportunity for forward-thinking Americans to build something totally new and scrap the tired old scripts of what work has looked like for nearly a century.

Speaking of dying institutions, let's talk college!

Old School

Eighteen is a strange age. You go from a child focused on homework, sports, dating, dances, and friends to being able to vote, smoke, get tatted up, and sign your entire life away. Between Algebra II and making after-school plans, you're determining your career path without a large breadth of knowledge or deeper understanding of your options. For most of us, college is an afterthought, a social experiment in getting laid, not the next clear step toward the career we've prudently outlined in our minds.

So, you fill out applications and write college admissions letters that feel more like optimistic letters to Santa Claus, sugarcoated in hopeful naivete. You wake up on the proverbial Christmas morning to unwrap your acceptance letter, and your life is forever changed.

Four years later you graduate with a degree in Eighteenth-Century Lesbian Poetry, eighty-thousand dollars in debt, and a shiny new job at Panera Bread—that is, if you're lucky to find a job at all. Turns out, the unemployment rate for young college graduates is higher than that of the general population—plus about 41 percent of recent college graduates are working jobs that don't even need a college degree.[7]

Don't get me wrong. Education and higher learning are amazing things. They open up the mind to new ideas and new ways to think. But the educational institution? It's swindling all of us.

As you may recall from chapter two, progressives are obsessed with the institution of learning. This makes perfect sense from their point of view, as colleges now exist to create conformity of thought— teaching students *what* to think and not *how* to think (there's a reason Bill Gates, Steve Jobs, Mark Zuckerberg, and Michael Dell didn't graduate). So if you're trying to beat the robots from taking your job by becoming a robot, maybe college really is your best bet!

This is why Peter Thiel announced in 2010 at a San Francisco tech conference, that he'd pay $100,000 to twenty people under the age of twenty to drop out of school, move to the Bay Area, and work on anything they wanted for two years. According to Thiel, a college diploma is "a dunce cap in disguise."[8] Instead of shucking out a small fortune to learn what's already been learned, he wanted to jumpstart a renaissance of Big Tech breakthroughs that contemporary Silicon Valley lacked. He also wanted to prove college's counterproductiveness—stimulating thinking by telling young people what to think and forcing them to spend money to make money.

The website for the Thiel Foundation presents it like this: "College can be good for learning about what's been done before, but it can also discourage you from doing something new." In other words, schools teach about innovations while innovators innovate.

Interestingly enough, more and more companies no longer require a college degree. As of 2020, Google, Apple, and IBM were among those that didn't require one. It's not just big companies though. In fact, most small-business owners in the US don't have a four-year degree.[9] This is because innovation and entrepreneurship typically require people who think differently.

The reality? We've *outgrown* higher education. When everybody has a degree, nobody needs a degree. When everyone is being taught the same thing, no one is thinking differently. There are definitely careers that warrant going to school (I mean, I do not want an untrained or formally uneducated heart surgeon), but it seems that similar to our workweeks, our entire career trajectories need a bit of an overhaul.

The good news is I think most of us are starting to get that. When white-collar workers were sent home to work indefinitely, students were sent home to do the same. Suddenly, the best part of college was stolen from them: the live, on-campus experience. And I mean stolen quite literally. Harvard, which costs upward of $70,000 a year, failed to repay room and board in full for the 2020 school year, despite dorm rooms sitting empty.

Students sat in their high school bedrooms, listening to lectures on Zoom, with this underlying feeling of *Am I missing something?*

In May 2020, I chatted with Mike Rowe, who knows a thing or two about the workforce as the host of Discovery Channel's *Dirty Jobs* and *Someone's Gotta Do It*. He put it like this:

> I watched on YouTube a lecture from MIT for *free*—the same lecture that would cost thousands of dollars. When the dust settles, higher education will be revealed for the luxury brand that it truly is. When you take away all the stuff that has nothing to do with learning and connecting, you're going to be left with a breathtakingly overpriced product.

If higher learning was really about higher learning, we'd all be talking about the plethora of good and cheap resources available. The minute you realize what you have free or inexpensive access to is the minute your eyes are opened to the university racket. A ten-dollar book can provide much more than ten-thousand-dollar tuition if you actually read the book. Plus, the internet is full of free lectures by some of the greatest thinkers and educators of our time. People like Thomas Sowell, Larry Elder, and Jordan Peterson are just a click away, and with modern technology, you can actually reach out to them directly (and even outside of office hours!).

Alas, higher learning is not about learning—it's about brainwashing, conformity, money, and scaring young minds into thinking that there is only one way to move through the world. I promise you, the history books are not filled with those who took the oft traveled, obligatory road. It's filled with innovators, nonconformists, and free-thinking individuals.

Like the cultural anthropologist Margaret Mead said, "My grandmother wanted me to have an education, so she kept me out of school."

So, to the young, future American on the precipice of making a life-changing decision: Really think through what you want in this life. Will going to school really get you any closer to the thing you want to be or that life you want to lead? Or could saving your money and watching a YouTube lecture teach you more than you'd ever get at that $40,000-a-year university? If you're a forward-thinking parent, sit down with your child and talk through that post-high school stage. Don't rush him or her to make a decision or to take the tired old path because you fear your child will fall behind. Maybe instead of shelling out $100,000 to a college that's going to brainwash your kids, consider giving them a down payment on their first home instead.

To the modern American in positions to hire and lead: Don't feed the system—hire based on skill, ability, personality, and uniqueness over credentials. Hire the person who is best for the job and not strictly for who has the perfect resume and impressive college degree, or for who will meet your company's equity quotas. Look for those candidates who have a work ethic and a story to tell and not necessarily to those who got duped by the failing institutions and dream-crushing systems.

And as far as the rest of ya, remember: True education is a lifelong pursuit. Don't think it's done once you've graduated or once you've got a job. Keep learning, keep absorbing, and keep taking in new experiences—and do it *your* way.

That's Rich

At the start of 2021, I found myself on the other side of life when I was talking to one of our interns, Phoenix. Yes, that's his real name—it's not just some exceptionally hot, low-humidity city. His internship was wrapping up so we sat down to chat through next steps. He was still in college and he was trying to decide if he wanted to continue his formal education or accept a full-time job to work for me doing production work.

"Well, what do you want to do with your life?" I asked him.

"I want to be *you*."

It was one of those grounding moments. Suddenly, I was forced to look back at all the strange puzzle pieces of my life. I didn't become Jon Stewart (thank god) and I'm not hosting *The Tonight Show* (and would literally laugh in their faces if it was offered to me but not because they're funny), nor am I doing regular stand-up gigs in comedy clubs. But I got my own show and I've traveled the world and spoken in front of hundreds of thousands of people making them laugh. I wake up each morning feeling purposeful, excited to work and make a living.

When you're young—whether you're a twenty-three-year-old assistant manager at Electronics Boutique in 1999 or a nineteen-year-old intern who is contemplating next steps in 2021—you're desperately looking for the puzzle box that shows you the end result so you can start putting something perfect and pristine together. But that's just not how life goes. Instead, we're handed jagged edges and uneven pieces and have to try to see how it all fits into the bigger picture.

I told Phoenix I'd be happy to give him a job without having graduated, but felt he needed to have some moments off the beaten path first. Plus, frankly, I needed someone who didn't want to "be me" but enjoyed doing the organizational work that needed to be done. So I told him that while I'd always be here to support him, and that the offer still stood, I thought it'd be better for him to move on and take some risks.

If I were to tell younger me what I know now, he would feel thrilled with how his life would come together albeit a bit surprised. The thing is, I'd never tell him. Because if he would have known, he wouldn't have taken all those risks—starting secret live-audience television shows, opening clubs, leaving networks, going solo, and building several successful companies. And if younger me hadn't made all those mistakes, then this career—and more importantly life—would have never come together the way that it did.

9

BE A HERO,
NOT A COMRADE

Some cause happiness wherever they go; others whenever they go.

Oscar Wilde

Luck of the Irish

It was July 14, 2018, and Jordan Peterson and I were in Dublin, Ireland, on what felt like our millionth stop on the *12 Rules for Life* tour. We had already been to London, Amsterdam, Stockholm, Melbourne, and every single major city in the US, and while each day was an adventure of its own, every day also bore striking resemblance to the one preceding.

Every single day was travel, media hits, hotel check-ins, more media hits, and stage prep. Every night, we would go to some restaurant where I would order the local fare and Jordan, ever the disciplined diner, would order the best cut of steak with just a sprinkling of salt. Every night, we'd head over to the theater and start preparing in the green room. I'd go out onstage, crack a few jokes, and introduce him, and while the lecture he gave each night was different, the audience's reaction was always the same: complete awe of the colossal intellectual feat they had just witnessed.

After such an incredibly full day, both physically and mentally, by the time the meet and greet rolled around at the end of the night, Jordan would still shake every person's hand and ask their name and where they were from.

It would be around 1:00 a.m. by the time the whole shindig wrapped up. We would then head back to the green room and debrief. His wife, Tammy, would join us and he'd always eagerly ask her thoughts.

On this night, similar to all the other nights, Jordan, Tammy, David, our tour manager, John, and I chatted for a while and then gathered our things to head out of the Olympia Theater. We slipped out the inconspicuous side door all the major theaters have that opens onto some back alley.

As we stepped out we saw two men huddled together in the shadows, sounding distressed and mumbling something in a thick Irish accent. Homeless people? Drug dealers? Prostitutes?

When they heard the door close behind us, the two men looked up and started running toward us. Certain we were about to get mugged, I prepared for the worst. But as they got closer, I noticed that one man was in his sixties and the other in his twenties, and that they had been crying.

Wiping tears from their eyes, they started to tell us their story. They were father and son and had a huge falling out about five years ago. On their own personal timelines, they had both separately bought Jordan's book, *12 Rules for Life,* and began fixing up

their lives. Separately, they had attended the show, and as the thousands of people exited the theater that evening, they happened to
notice each other from across the mezzanine, walked toward each
other, and—right then and there, after so much time and so much
heartache—made amends.

Jordan started crying. Tammy started crying. John started
crying. I started crying. This kind of deeply human moment wasn't
rare. In fact, it was a nightly occurrence and was hands down my favorite thing about touring. All across our travels, from all over the
world, we would hear stories of people's lives being changed—stories
we would have never heard if we hadn't taken the time to shake hands,
get to know our fellow humans, and listen to the stories they wanted
to share.

But this father-son story in Dublin stood out to me in particular
because they had sworn to never speak to each other again. It was the
fact that they were living totally separate lives but were still on some
similar trajectory, the fact that it took being open to bigger ideas that
made space for them to heal and repair, and the fact that on that night
we saw a father and son reconcile and a family reunite. It's amazing—
the moment they began to focus on themselves and try to better their
own individual lives, was the moment they began creating a healthy
foundation for mutual understanding and true connection.

You see, the story of the individual is also a story of how that individual fits into the grander narrative—starting with the family and
then reverberating out to one's friends, local community, country,
and ultimately, to the entire world. When individuals are healthier,
the family can be healthier, and in turn, society becomes healthier.

While we may exist as individuals independent of one another,
we can still be deeply connected to one another. Sure, someone can

choose to live a selfish, disconnected life all alone in their giant mansion at the top of the hill—and that's totally fine, I suppose—but, my god, you miss out when you don't really connect with the people in your orbit and beyond. Whether it's shaking hands with people on foreign streets or reconciling with your long-lost family member, real, true, honest-to-goodness human connection is critical toward that lofty goal of the pursuit of happiness.

Author James Truslow Adams coined the term *American Dream* in his 1931 book, *The Epic of America.* In it he wrote, "The dream has not been a dream of material plenty, though that has doubtlessly counted heavily. It has been a dream of being able to grow to fullest development as a man and woman, unhampered by the barriers which had slowly been erected in the older civilizations, unrepressed by social orders which had developed for the benefit of classes rather than for the simple human being of any and every class."

When the American Enterprise Institute conducted a survey in 2019 to unpack the American Dream, it presented participants with eight distinct factors that could be considered components of the Dream. They were asked to rate the eight factors in accordance with their personal opinions. The eight factors, from highest valued components to lowest were: to have freedom of choice in how to live one's life; to have a good family life; to retire comfortably; to own a home; to have a successful career; to have a better quality of life than your parents; to make valuable contributions to your community; and to become wealthy.

The results tell an interesting story: 85 percent of Americans said that "to have freedom of choice in how to live one's life" was the highest valued component, followed closely by 83 percent choosing "to have a good family life." Only 16 percent felt "to become wealthy" was essential.[1]

The American Dream and happiness in general isn't about money and wealth or fancy homes and job titles. It's about freedom. It's about family. From there, all else follows and all else reverberates. When freedom is at the core, humans can live out their lives in their own unique way, unobstructed by societal expectations. Yes, each life will look wildly different and unique, and so will those families.

The 2.5 kids with a golden retriever and white picket fence may be the dream for someone but not someone else. Although we need to protect the nuclear family at its core, we've also got to be okay with it evolving, advancing, and looking different across the human spectrum. I mean, the word *nuclear* does come from the Latin word for nut, *nux*, which makes a hell of a lot of sense—a lot of families seem pretty damn nutty. But the premise is valid: from a nut, things can grow, and from a family, so can the individual, and eventually, an entire community can flourish.

Community versus Collectivism

Have you ever noticed that there are no families in a dystopian novel?

There's a reason for that.

A totalitarian regime knows the one thing it can't compete against is humans having real human connection in a place that is safe for them to personally develop into strong, free-thinking individuals.

Instead what you have at the center of each dystopian story is a lone protagonist, isolated in his or her own adventure and desperate for human connection. *The Matrix* has Neo, *Fahrenheit 451* has Guy Montag, and *1984* has Winston Smith.

In *1984*, Winston has a vague recollection of his family from his childhood and remembers his wife, Katharine, who suddenly disappeared after the revolution. No spouse, no family, but it's okay—he has his job at the Ministry of Truth and works for the government of Oceania, called the Party. Super fun! His duties? Revising history by altering facts to fit the propaganda of Big Brother. ("War is peace; freedom is slavery; ignorance is strength.") Anything that doesn't conform to the ideology? Wiped clean. (Hint: that's what happened to his childhood memories . . . and probably Katharine. And if I remember the story correctly, pretty sure they kicked him off Twitter.)

Naturally, Big Brother doesn't allow members of the party to have families. They can't even get laid! Instead Big Brother promotes sexlessness among the women in the Party, who avoid making themselves attractive (looking like a bunch of angry third-wave feminists).

The lack of family, affection, and human connection would mean a lot of lonely people. But worry not—the Party fills that void for you! What was once love for your family becomes love of the Party. Who needs a biological brother if you have Big Brother? And if you don't love Big Brother, other citizens will turn you in. Because duty! Because love!

But Big Brother doesn't exist. Big Brother is not an actual flesh-and-blood human being; Winston Smith was. Big Brother is an icon, a mascot, a false personification of the Party, intended to incite love and fear—"It *depicted* simply an enormous face, more than a meter wide: the face of a man of about forty-five, with a heavy black mustache." I realize as I write this, I am months away from turning forty-five . . . I don't have a mustache though so you can still trust me.

Winston tries to retain his individuality against the collective identity by doing "radical" things like keeping a diary and finding a lady friend. He skips out on going to the Community Center or participating in social groups and instead wanders working-class neighborhoods and sits and thinks in his apartment—dangerous stuff that the Party calls *ownlife*.

I won't give away the rest. Although, I guess, what I said in an earlier chapter still stands: there's *got* to be an expiration date on spoiler alerts (and we're pretty much living in it anyways). But the point is made: the best way for a totalitarian regime to keep its power is to strip you of your individuality. For Oceania, the fictional setting of *1984*, this started with the destruction of the family. When you remove the family—when you remove a deep, personal, private, nucleus—the government can step in and take control. When you don't have people to connect with deeply, you lose your ability to remain separate from collectivist thinking.

This isn't just intellectual. There is a reason you think about your family more than you do other people. There's a reason that absent parents can leave long-lasting emotional scars. There's a reason that after a falling out, you can't stop thinking about your son or daughter.

That isn't to say that other groups in your life aren't important. You can be in a knitting club or on a basketball team and love your fellow knitters and teammates very much. But, fundamentally, these people aren't your family. For instance, if someone on your basketball team died without warning—someone you were very close to and saw weekly—you would probably still be affected differently than if your brother died, even if you hadn't spoken to him for years.

It's why I hate the lefty slang term *fam*. Sorry, Twitter lady, you are *not* my family.

Thus, woke progressivism continues to lead a similar charge of the Orwellian disintegration of the family, following a course laid out by cultural Marxists.

Take the Black Lives Matter movement for instance.

There are in essence two Black Lives Matter. First is the *idea* that black lives matter. Of course black lives matter. I even said it before in this very book! How much more proof do you need? I support this in all ways, shapes, and forms. We should have a healthy dialogue where many different people can come to the table to discuss alternative reformative solutions, experiences, or ways to move forward. I for one am always a fan of healthy, balanced exchanges.

Second, is the Black Lives Matter *organization*. Admittedly, I am less thrilled about this one. It was founded by Patrisse Cullors, Alicia Garza, and Opal Tometi, all of whom have roots in Marxism. Don't take it from me, a white, cis, man. Take it from one of the founders herself. In 2015, Cullors said of the organization, "The first thing, I think, is that we actually do have an ideological frame. Myself and Alicia in particular are trained organizers . . . we are trained Marxists. We are super-versed on, sort of, ideological theories."[2]

Well, Patrisse, I'm super-versed on, sort of, debunking this nonsense.

This is dangerous stuff. Marxists believed the "long march through the institutions" (the Marxist slogan coined by communist student activist Rudi Dutschke) was the best route to taking power in society. This "march" would be a gradual process of radicalizing and destabilizing the middle class, the nuclear family, and individualism as a philosophy and a way of life.

Sure enough, the Black Lives Matter organization had a "What We Believe" page on its website, but during the summer of 2020, as the movement gained traction and people flocked to the website, staff at *The Washington Examiner* discovered the page had been removed.[3]

What once read: "We disrupt the Western-prescribed nuclear family structure requirement by supporting each other as extended families and 'villages' that collectively care for one another, especially our children, to the degree that mothers, parents, and children are comfortable." Now says: "404 Not Found. We cannot find the page you are looking for."[4]

I'm not saying that the "collective village" intentions are necessarily bad. What with fathers walking out on families left and right, the desire to fill that hole for children is in some ways understandable. But this is the very reason we need to put more power, more weight, and more responsibility toward supporting the individual and the nuclear family, rather than stripping them away with perverse Marxist ideologies that basically want to tear everything down and replace the individual and family with the collective, the state, or the Party.

Let's look at another example.

From 1979 to 2015, the Chinese Communist Party burrowed its way into the family, establishing the "one-child" policy. This edict was a way to maintain population control and it placed limits on the number of children a family living in China could have. Years before the policy went into effect, CCP Chairman Mao Zedong explained why it was necessary for the state to have control over the family at a procreation level:

> (Re)production needs to be planned. In my view, humankind
> is completely incapable of managing itself. It has plans for
> production in factories, for producing cloth, tables and chairs,

and steel, but there is no plan for producing humans. This is anarchism—no governing, no organization and no rules. This government perhaps needs to have a special ministry—what about a ministry of birth control? Or perhaps establishing a commission, as part of the government?[5]

We all know how the one-child policy went. Some have estimated that 30 to 60 million girls went missing in China—many possibly killed in the womb or just after birth, due to a preference for sons over daughters. All because the government stuck its nose somewhere it never belonged. Suddenly, what was once a living, breathing, individual human being is a mere resource to be used for the collective agenda, no different than cloth, tables, chairs, and steel.

This is what happens when the collective replaces the family and family matters become political ones. This is what happens when we rely on the system and the government to fix our deeply human problems rather than empowering the individual to step up to the plate and fix their shit.

If *1984* wasn't your cup of tea, let's put it in *Brave New World* dystopian terms: "Everyone belongs to everyone else." This is what cultural Marxism looks like.

Individualism says the opposite: you don't belong to anyone, and if you did, you sure as hell don't belong to *everyone*. If you belong to anyone it's your personal family—those that love you and care for you, not some monolithic, collective body.

If the only flaw of individualism and the nuclear family is that it prioritizes "your" people, then I am A-OK with that. Because imagine if all people took care of *their* spouses and *their* children. Fathers might stick around and fix their lives up and spouses might take into consideration their partner's needs. Imagine if everyone supported the people they were journeying through life with first—helped them think and grow and develop into fully fleshed individuals. Those people eventually go out into the world as good citizens and good colleagues, eventually becoming contributing members of a community not because they're *forced* to but because they really do care.

That, my friends, is the difference between a community and a collective. A community is made up of unique individuals all looking out primarily for themselves while at the same time contributing to the greater good by helping the world around them. A collective is just a bunch of replaceable, expendable, interchangeable people with one hive mind. The community is made up of individuals who want civil discourse, the collective is composed of the ones who drown out conversation with mindless chants and uniforms.

In other words: a community is the Jedi Council, a collective is the Stormtroopers. (Sorry, I couldn't resist making just one more *Star Wars* reference!)

So much that is wrong with society comes down to collectivist thinking, viewing someone as a member of the Party, and not as Winston Smith. We've lumped everybody together and started playing this terrible game of identity politics, grouping people together via immutable traits rather than treating people as individuals. It's like a sick and twisted version of Red Rover, inviting people to come over just to knock them down. That doesn't accomplish anything and that sure as hell ain't fun.

Yet, that's exactly what intersectionality does (which, as we know, is another key tenet of the Black Lives Matter organization and the woke movement at large). Intersectionality is the archnemesis of community. We've been taught through woke propaganda to embrace intersectionality as the good guy that will bring us all together. It's not uniting, however, but rather dividing us all, even the individual itself.

Intersectionality can be explained like this: If you are a male, heterosexual, cisgender, able-bodied, native-born American, you're privileged. But if you're *not* white then your oppression is limited only to your non-whiteness. One oppression just isn't good enough! So what if you're not white but you're also not male? Now that place where your non-whiteness and your non-maleness intersect is where you feel the heaviest weight of the oppression. But what if you're not white and not male and not heterosexual? Oy vey. The oppression on you is even worse because you have these three intersections of oppression. And what if you're not white, not male, not heterosexual, and not cisgender? So now you're a black-trans-male-lesbian, I guess—I don't know, I lost track—but now there are four intersections of oppression and you've hit the woke jackpot. Congratulations.

Instead of accepting yourself as a robust, three-dimensional individual (who may fit all of the above descriptions, and that is great!), you are separating and relegating yourself to a subgroup that cares *only* about your characteristics and not about who you really are (talk about some sexist, homophobic, racist, transphobic bullshit).

And don't get me wrong. If the government started cracking down on you because you're a black-trans-male-lesbian, I will be out there by your side every day. I would be your biggest ally. But most of the time this isn't about real oppression. It's people choosing to be victims and sub-characters rather than the protagonists in their own life stories.

If you're not the hero of your own story, then you're more than likely a part of someone else's and the role you get cast in is probably not the one you would pick. In our travels, Jordan would often mention a quote by Carl Jung, "People don't have ideas. Ideas have people."

Consider that for a minute. When people are possessed by an ideology—Marxism, communism, intersectionality, whatever—each of them has the exact same idea. If all the people have the same idea, what makes you think that *they* have the idea at all? Unless you can understand that it's very possible for ideas to have people, we can't understand how a dystopia takes shape in real life. When a collective or a monolithic, unthinking group of people take hold of an idea, they suddenly start to act that idea out without totally understanding the repercussions. What happens? Oceania feels less and less like fiction, Maoist China is birthed (or doesn't birth), and American cities burn in the name of tolerance and diversity.

Avoiding these types of consequences is why it's so important to have your own story. Be a self-reliant individual, not a member of the mob. If you're without your own story, you'll no doubt wake up to find yourself to be some strange sub-character in some strange subgroup in some strange subplot that you never wanted to be in. You'll look around and suddenly see that it wasn't a comedy, grand epic, or a fairy tale, but a tragedy with you as some nameless victim.

Does anyone know the names of the runners who followed Forrest Gump? But everyone remembers Forrest Gump.

Once you become the protagonist of your own plot, then you become a hero of the story around you.

What does a good protagonist look like? What does a fully developed individual look like? What does a hero look like? It looks like a dad not walking away from his family, a partner putting a loved one's needs first, a friend listening to your thoughts without early judgment, an employee working hard, a boss being a good leader, a neighbor helping out a neighbor. Sometimes just going home and hugging your spouse and kid is a better and faster way to change the world. Because if we aren't good spouses, good parents, good kids, good colleagues, good neighbors, and good individuals, how can we expect the world to be a decent place?

And sometimes you're not going to be the hero. There are times you will fail, slip up, pack it in, or entertain notions of turning to the dark side. But until the story is over, this is the messy middle where we exist. This is just what it means to be a human, and empowering the individual human is the best possible path toward building a strong community and better world. It certainly won't look like utopia, but better yet, it won't look like dystopia.

Love Thy Neighbor

If you were to watch the news, read the papers, scroll through Twitter, and listen to the politicians, you would hear a pretty depressing story about America's future—one of doom, gloom, division, and despair. But meanwhile, in a place called reality, things are looking pretty damn good in America (if we can keep it). At least that's the finding of journalist James Fallows, who spent years traveling to the most unknown and unheard of towns in Middle America—from Mississippi, Kansas, inland California, South Dakota, and "rust belt" Pennsylvania—most of which were known more for a natural disaster or school shooting than as travel destinations. In his 2018

Atlantic article, Fallows opens his findings with, "I have seen the future, and it is in the United States."

His futuristic vision of American grandeur comes down to one key factor: the local level. These towns in Middle America were happy and thriving with no central planners nor federally elected politicians—just populated with people invested in the town they lived in. Fallows writes, "Even as national politics induces trust and despair, most polls show rising faith in local governance."[6] Fallows didn't get everything right in his article (Orange Man bad!), but he hit the nail on the head with the future of America's flourishing being rooted at a local level.

In the modern world, local ties are often overshadowed by abstract, global ones—but in the last few years we've learned that our "global" alliances are generally pretty useless when it really counts. I mean, what did the UN or WHO actually do during the coronavirus other than to send out often conflicting mixed messages? Being aware of international and national politics is critical, but being plugged into your community at a local, nuclear level is even more vital for the country and your personal future.

Again, the individualist's story starts private and moves outward—from individual, to family, to local community, then to country, and last, to the world. That's the order of pragmatic priority. It's not selfish; it's just smart.

When you've got yourself and your family happy and healthy, step outside your front door. Take a look at the very street you live on. Do you know your neighbors' names?

To be fair, as I write this now, neither do I.

I moved to a neighborhood the summer of 2020, smack-dab in the middle of quarantine. Under different circumstances, I'd usually be the guy who knocks on my new neighbors' front doors and invites them over for a big ol' dinner party. But being in L.A., it's a grab bag of whether or not the people would turn you in for not social distancing, and being in this modern dystopia means that most likely they'd google me and then hate me for something that I never even said.

I wasn't always the friendly neighborhood guy. When I lived in New York, I lived in the same tiny apartment for years, with walls as thin as wheat crackers, and I knew my neighbors' sex lives more than I knew their names. In fact, I lived above a little person who liked to get gang banged, but that's a story for another book.

Being a good neighbor is something I've had to actively work on every single day. As I walk Clyde down our street, I try to wave to everyone I see, and during the spread of coronavirus, I tried to shake hands with everyone I hated (kidding!). With all of the future conditions—technological, social, and political—it's going to make it increasingly hard to make real, flesh-and-blood human connections. When the entire system is designed around having less human interaction, we'll have to make it an intentional effort to connect with one another meaningfully.

Take a look outside your front door again. Is there trash lining the streets? Is there an empty lot filled with junk? In the previous neighborhood David and I moved from, everyone left their garbage cans out on the street every day, so we did too. I didn't really think of it all that much at the time, but when we moved to our new neighborhood, I realized how nice it was to look out the window and see clean streets without giant trash cans every five feet. So I brought in our trash cans—I didn't want to be the only resident leaving his shit on the curb. That next day, I realized, "Well, heck, it does look nice without a trash can out front." Small-scale individualism naturally making the neighborhood a little nicer.

It works in reverse as well. If you're the person who lowers the bar, eventually, over time, others might lower the bar too, and suddenly the streets are filled with trash and property values plummet.

As you move beyond your street, observe your neighborhood, look at your town, your city, your region, your state. Support as locally as possible. Buy from your local farmers. Eat at your local restaurants. Shop from your local stores and become a patron to your local artists. Invest in your community infrastructure. Shake hands with your neighbors, and remember, communities, not just individuals, need to be self-reliant.

Be an Entertainer, Not a Wine Mom

We've talked a lot about people in this book; how each unique individual can pursue happiness in a cuckoo, bananas world. We've talked a lot about ideas too; good ones, bad ones, and completely nonsensical ones. We've talked about varying and competing philosophies, ideologies, visions, and beliefs. But there is a physical thing—a place—where these things can come under one roof. There's a place where diverse ideas, philosophies, and people can come together, not in a way that collides but in a way that flourishes.

Your home.

Your home is a physical embodiment of your individuality and a proverbial training ground for how to be the person you want to be in the world outside its doors.

David and I bought our current house with the intention of hosting visitors and throwing parties as much as we possibly could. The irony was that we bought it at a time of travel bans and forbidden gatherings. And we followed those rules 100 percent. I mean, we would have *never* thrown a party with 100 people to eat pizza and drink wine when our beloved, faultless mayor, Eric Garcetti, told us not to! What kind of citizen do you think I am?! (Thanks again to everyone that came.)

For me, there is truly no greater joy than preparing for a dinner party. I put on my favorite music—usually Frank Sinatra or Frankie Valli. (I guess I have something for Franks?) We'll straighten up the house and David will make an incredible dinner. Sometimes we'll go all out and get tomahawk steaks and I'll slap 'em on the grill while he makes cocktails and sides.

As he makes the drinks and picks the music, I'll set the table. Oddly enough, this has become one of my favorite parts of the night whether or not people are coming over. After a long day of arguing with lunatics on Twitter, to set the table, fold some napkins, and light candles adds some calm and order to my day. Instead of ordering in and eating out of a plastic container or cardboard box as I sit at my desk, cooking a meal and sitting at a clean table keeps my evenings somewhat sacred. It's not about having British etiquette school–style behavior circa 1920, although, sometimes you'll definitely find me humming the theme song to *Downton Abbey* as I lay down the forks and knives. Entertaining is about enjoying the smallest and most forgotten parts of daily life and creating an experience for you and for others.

Being an individual really comes down to knowing what makes you *you*. Know what you like, know your favorite music, have a go-to cocktail or entrée that you can make when your friends come over. Fill your home with art—not because it's trendy or because the art institution told you that's what has value—but because the artwork somehow inspires you.

It has nothing to do with how nice your home is, but everything to do with how much it represents you and creates a space that people want to spend time in. Inviting people into your home to discuss, relax, and gather is the balm for the daily minutia of politicization. Light some candles, dim the lights, make a cheese board, pour some wine, display the good soap. These little things can go a long way, and trust me, nobody hates the person who throws a good party.

When hosting a dinner party, I try to always do a few things: Make a toast. Have everyone introduce themselves. Break up the couples. Then I try to keep to one engaging conversation rather than to have a bunch of mini conversations. This strategy reduces the social anxiety for some and usually elevates the conversation. You don't have to force some grandiose, groundbreaking discussion either—just ask, "Hey, anything particular on anyone's mind?" Somebody almost always speaks up. And if you just hear crickets, well, maybe you need new friends.

So, create a space that fosters conversation and remember: echo chambers don't force you to interrogate your own beliefs and censorship doesn't cultivate personal growth; conversation does. Through a culture of conversation we can come together again, not as a collective but as a community, all of us a part of the diverse human family.

While this hyperpoliticization isn't going away anytime soon (short of sending me and you to the gulag), it doesn't mean that you can't be better while in the middle of it. When Big Government knocks on your door or that little computer in your pocket feels too irresistible to ignore, remember you have a personal responsibility to be the best authentic version of yourself while being present in the now. So know yourself, cherish every moment no matter how small, love your family well, take care of the people around you, and get to know as many people as you possibly can. Then invite them all under one roof for a big party. Host people and make it a point to make them feel invited and welcome (even if you think their ideas are totally looney tunes). Be willing to be the one who listens before they speak. I'm telling you, this attentive act might be the rarest of all gems these days.

If you do one thing, do this: hold fast to your values but don't let that keep you from inviting people who disagree with you into your home (you might even be related to some of them). Create an environment for individuals—diverse, conflicting, messy *individuals*—to gather and create a community. Because a community of individuals creates a wide tent, and it's that kind of tent that, over time, brings people out of the scorching heat of the progressive Left into the cool shade of rationality. It's the kind of tent we need to bring people from all walks of life so as to build a better future.

And one more thing, my dear reader: create a life worthy of celebration—cause that's what this whole wild ride is all about. It's about being a vibrant, free-thinking individual, and it's about surviving, yes, but more important, *thriving* in our dystopian future.

Conclusion

WHAT ARE YOU GOING TO DO?

t's some unknown time in the future. After a civil war broke out, the concept of time was considered oppressive, so along with the books, everyone burned all the calendars and clocks, which is great for sleeping in but not for waking up.

The civil war consisted of two groups: one who wanted to conserve and one who wanted to destroy. Eventually, the group that wanted to conserve went underground to their bunkers to live out their individual lives. Some still discussed the truths and complexities of life, while some buried their heads like ostriches, but by going underground, they left the group who wanted to destroy.

You're one of the few who peeks their head above the rubble to see what's going on in the world above you, however. And while you were glad to have had your canned beans and canned tuna to survive, you woke up one morning to realize you're surviving, sure, but you're not thriving. You want more than this. You know deep down this is no way to live.

So you crawl out of your underground bunker and start to build your house on firm land. You build it thoughtfully, making it yours. Eventually, you invite your friends from the bunkers and when seeing that you're safe, they join you for dinners and gatherings. Your life inspires others to crawl out of their introspective bunkers and build more and more aboveground. You're all still afraid of that group who wants to destroy the community you're creating, but even some of those from the opposition see what you're building and join as refugees, because they also know, deep down, that there is a better way to move forward. Over time a whole movement is forged—you build beautiful homes, significant institutions, and create meaningful art.

This is not a new story. It's the story of "Plato's Cave" that we explored in chapter three. Guess what? It's even the story of America's founding—that of a bunch of courageous individuals creating, building, and paving a new way forward in the middle of destructive authoritarian control.

America's founders gave us the tools—the ethos and the paperwork—we needed to thrive, but over time, America has begun to revert to the ways its colonists were trying to escape in the first place.

By shamefully rewriting our country's history as one of woke oppression and revising our Constitution in their favor, the new, progressive Left is dangerously close to turning what was once the "land of the free" into a wasteland. Meanwhile, conservatives are divided as to how to fight back.

Progressives will always see our Constitution as laughable and irrelevant—and they become more radical as the decades pass. Need I remind you of the moment during the third Democratic debate leading into the 2020 general election when Joe Biden clashed with Kamala Harris onstage over their antigun positions. In response to Joe Biden's claim that some executive bans on guns are unconstitutional, Harris said, "Hey Joe—instead of saying, 'No we can't' let's say, 'Yes we can.'" Joe is of the old world, when there was still some power Democrats couldn't have. Kamala represents our current world—and where the future is headed: one where nothing matters . . . nothing but power.

The woke progressives want to *destroy* America.

The rest of us need to *save* America.

That's why we, the only remaining force for sanity and truth in this country, need to *build*. Who will keep our unique values of life, liberty, equality, and happiness at heart while they pave a new way forward—a way out of the civil war, amid the despotic giants, and into another period of enlightenment? Who will keep an individualist spirit of self-reliance and creativity?

You will.

So, what are you going to do? That's the big question. Are you going to keep chugging along, trying not to rock your little tugboat, or are you going to break the cable and set sail on your own adventure? Are you going to seek out that fundamental American right to life, liberty, and the pursuit of happiness?

Because that's also what this whole American experiment is all

about: it's *the pursuit of happiness*. It may not look the same for everyone. Some may have it better than others, but everyone can shoot for
a life that's better than the one they inherited. And while you may
not change the world, can you change your life for the better, even
just marginally? Can you make one choice today toward bettering
your own life?

I know it may be difficult at times to see the silver lining in this
dystopian nightmare. Because who knows what the future holds?
Maybe it's going to be a disaster where the Left's delusions throw us
into a civil war. Maybe, there will be more pandemics, more lockdowns, more riots, and more crises. Maybe the giants of Big Tech and
Big Government will garner more and more authoritarian power.

Or maybe, just *maybe*, some really great things will happen.
Maybe we'll remember that America is an incredible place where we
all can be free, equal, and happy. Maybe we will create a society of
strong families and entrepreneurs. Maybe there will be robots and
jetpacks, and we'll feel like the Jetsons—everyone will be evolved,
authentic, and neighborly. (Although Mr. Spacely was a bit over-
bearing.)

No matter the future circumstances, wouldn't you want to be the
best version of yourself? Imagine if you were to do most of the things
we've explored in this book . . . what's the *worst* that would happen? If
the future is grim, you'll simply be prepared; and if the future looks
bright, well, you'll be even brighter (either way maybe your bunker
will look a little more aesthetically pleasing than it would have).
That's the new American Dream: living a life that's *yours* to live and
building a better future because of it.

We've reached the end, friends. We've learned some new stuff,
shared a couple laughs, maybe even shed a few tears (I know, some of

it was bleak!), but by reading this book, I hope you've found what I've found: how to be free and how to be happy. It won't come by following the woke mob or by being reliant on a crumbling system. It comes from being your own person.

Now that you hold the key, what are you going to do?

Acknowledgments

David, you not only got the Dedication of this book but also you're first in the Acknowledgments. Everything I'm able to accomplish is only possible because of the support, confidence, and space you give me to make things happen. There's nobody I'd rather be on this crazy ride with. (So now can we get that life-size Han Solo in Carbonite statue for the living room? C'mon, you know it's cool!)

To four great thinkers, who have helped shaped my worldview, inspired me to become a better man, and whom I'm proud to call friends: Glenn Beck and Larry Elder, Jordan Peterson, and Dennis Prager.

To Michael and Connor, who sit in the studio with me each and every day and make sure I know what I'm talking about, that I'm sitting up straight, and that my hair is just right. You guys can expense guacamole from Chipotle for as long as you work with me.

To the entire Penguin team, particularly Adrian Zackheim, who gave this book the green light in an incredibly uncertain time, and to my editor Helen Healey, who will one day be a publishing legend.

Everyone else who got acknowledged in the last book, those still count.

And finally, you. Yes, you . . . the person reading this right now. Your belief in me inspires my belief in these ideas and this country. For that I owe you endless thanks. So thank you. Now go out and get yourself something nice.

Notes

Introduction: Welcome to Dystopia

1. Gibson, Kate. "U.S. Gun Sales Surge to Record High in 2020." CBS News, Nov. 3, 2020. cbsnews.com/news/gun-sales-record-high-2020.

2. Wan, William. "For Months, He Helped His Son Keep Suicidal Thoughts at Bay. Then Came the Pandemic." *The Washington Post*, Nov. 23, 2020. washington post.com/health/2020/11/23/covid-pandemic-rise-suicides.

Chapter One: There Are No Other Letters in "I"

1. de Tocqueville, Alexis. *Democracy in America*. Translated by Henry Reeve. New York: Colonial Press, 1899, Project Gutenberg. gutenberg.org/files/815 /815-h/815-h.htm#link2H_4_0001.

2. "An Introduction to the Work of Tocqueville." Great Thinkers, Oct. 3, 2017. thegreatthinkers.org/tocqueville/introduction.

3. Ekins, Emily, et al. "Poll: 62% of Americans Say They Have Political Views They're Afraid to Share." Cato Institute, July 22, 2020. cato.org/survey -reports/poll-62-americans-say-they-have-political-views-theyre-afraid -share.

Chapter Two: Dismantling Systems of Structural Stupidity

1. Needham, Vicki. "Economy Adds 157K Jobs in July, Unemployment Down to 3.9 Percent." *The Hill*, Aug. 3, 2018. thehill.com/policy/finance/400220-july -jobs-report.

2. Freedlander, David. "A 1980s New York City Battle Explains Donald Trump's Candidacy." *Bloomberg*, Sept. 29, 2015. bloomberg.com/news/features/2015 -09-29/a-1980s-new-york-city-battle-explains-donald-trump-s-candidacy.

3. Daley, Suzanne. "Trump to Rebuild Wollman Rink at the City's Expense by Dec. 15." *The New York Times*, June 7, 1986. nytimes.com/1986/06/07/nyre gion/trump-to-rebuild-wollman-rink-at-the-city-s-expense-by-dec-15 .html.

4. Takahama, Elise. "Is Math Racist? New Course Outlines Prompt Conver- sations about Identity, Race in Seattle Classrooms." *The Seattle Times*, Oct. 15, 2019. seattletimes.com/education-lab/new-course-outlines-prompt-con- versations-about-identity-race-in-seattle-classrooms-even-in-math.

5. Watts, Marina. "In Smithsonian Race Guidelines, Rational Thinking and Hard Work Are White Values." *Newsweek*, July 17, 2020. newsweek.com/smithson ian-race-guidelines-rational-thinking-hard-work-are-white-values-1518333.

6. Pluckrose, Helen, and James Lindsay. *Cynical Theories: How Activist Scholar- ship Made Everything about Race, Gender, and Identity—and Why This Harms Everybody*. Durham, NC: Pitchstone, 2020: 237.

7. Kendi, Ibram X. *How to Be an Antiracist*. New York: One World, 2019: 9.

8. Shapiro, Ben. "The Problem of 'Anti-Racism.'" *Pittsburgh Post-Gazette*, July 4, 2020. post-gazette.com/opinion/Op-Ed/2020/07/04/Ben-Shapiro-anti-racism -problem-woke-crusade/stories/202007040004.

9. Kendi, *Be an Antiracist*, 189.

10. Ronald Reagan Presidential Foundation & Institute. Reagan Quotes and
    Speeches. "News Conference: Aug. 12, 1986." reaganfoundation.org/ronald
    -reagan/reagan-quotes-speeches/news-conference-1.

11. Lindsay, James, and Mike Nayna. "Postmodern Religion and the Faith of Social
    Justice." *New Discourses*, June 18, 2020. newdiscourses.com/2020/06/post
    modern-religion-faith-social-justice.

Chapter Three: Propaganda Protection

1. MacKay, Jory. "Screen Time Stats 2019: Here's How Much You Use Your Phone
   during the Workday." *RescueTime (blog)*, Mar. 21, 2019. blog.rescuetime.com
   /screen-time-stats-2018.

2. Lippmann, Walter. *Public Opinion*. Overland Park, KS: Digireads.com, 2020: 6.

3. Lippmann, Walter. "Journalism and the Higher Law." In *Liberty and the News*.
   mediastudies.press, 2020, (PDF), facsimile of chapter 1. New York: Harcourt,
   Brace and Howe, 1920. 10.32376/3f8575cb.6ab1dfab.

4. "2021 Edelman Trust Barometer." *Edelman*. edelman.com/trust/2021-trust
   -barometer.

5. Flood, Brian. "Trust in Mainstream Media on the Decline: 'The News Industry
   Is in Chaos.'" Fox News. Sept. 18, 2019. foxnews.com/media/decline-in-trust
   -of-the-media-is-troubling.

6. Gorokhova, Elena. *A Mountain of Crumbs: Growing Up behind the Iron Curtain*.
   London: Windmill Books, 2010: 181.

7. D'Souza, Deborah. "Netflix Doesn't Want to Talk about Binge-Watching." In-
   vestopedia, Nov. 2, 2018. investopedia.com.cach3.com/tech/netflix-obsessed
   -binge-watching-and-its-problem/index.html.

8. D'Souza, "Netflix Doesn't Want to Talk."

9. D'Souza, "Netflix Doesn't Want to Talk."

10. Levy, Ari. "Here's the Final Tally of Where Tech Billionaires Donated for the
    2020 Election." CNBC. Nov. 6, 2020. cnbc.com/2020/11/02/tech-billionaire
    -2020-election-donations-final-tally.html.

11. Levy, "Where Tech Billionaires Donated."

12. Shapiro, Ben. "Hollywood Wants Your Money . . . and Your Mind." PragerU, Dec. 18, 2017. prageru.com/video/hollywood-wants-your-moneyand-your-mind.

Chapter Four: The Declaration of Digital Independence

1. Southern, Lauren. "Patreon Banned My Account??" Uploaded on July 21, 2017, YouTube video, 07:29. youtube.com/watch?v=rtImwK5TI4g.

2. JackConteExtras. "Patreon CEO on Content Policy, Lauren Southern, and IGD." Uploaded on July 28, 2017, YouTube video, 10:47. youtube.com/watch?v=YmcK6GvgVPs.

3. Sargon of Akkad. "You Cannot Trust Patreon (#PatreonPurge 1)." Uploaded on Dec. 8, 2018, YouTube video, 29:07. youtube.com/watch?v=4ThPdCicEsg.

4. Weaver, Corinne, and Alec Schemmel. "Twitter, Facebook Censored Trump, Campaign 65 Times, Leave Biden Untouched." *Newsbusters*, Oct. 19, 2020. newsbusters.org/blogs/free-speech/corinne-weaver/2020/10/19/twitter-facebook-censored-trump-campaign-65-times-leave.

5. Bond, Shannon. "Facebook and Twitter Limit Sharing 'New York Post' Story about Joe Biden." NPR, Oct. 14, 2020. npr.org/2020/10/14/923766097/facebook-and-twitter-limit-sharing-new-york-post-story-about-joe-biden.

6. Lovelace, Ryan. "ACLU Raises Concerns amid Trump Twitter Ban." *The Washington Times*. Jan. 8, 2021. washingtontimes.com/news/2021/jan/8/aclu-raises-concerns-amid-trump-twitter-ban.

7. Cao, Sissi, and Jordan Zakarin. "Big Tech and CEOs Poured Millions into the Election. Here's Who They Supported." Observer Media, Nov. 2, 2020. observer.com/2020/11/big-tech-2020-presidential-election-donation-breakdown-ranking.

8. "Top Spenders: Lobbying Client and Total Spent." *OpenSecrets.org*. opensecrets.org/federal-lobbying/top-spenders?cycle=2020.

9. Samuels, David. "Is Big Tech Merging with Big Brother? Kinda Looks Like It." *Wired*, Jan. 23, 2019. wired.com/story/is-big-tech-merging-with-big-brother-kinda-looks-like-it.

10. "Announcing the New AWS Secret Region." *AWS Public Sector* (blog), Nov. 20, 2017. aws.amazon.com/blogs/publicsector/announcing-the-new-aws-secret-region.

11. Selyukh, Alina. "Amazon's Grand Search for 2nd Headquarters Ends with Split: NYC and D.C. Suburb." NPR, Nov. 13, 2018. npr.org/2018/11/13/66564 6050/amazons-grand-search-for-2nd-headquarters-ends-with-split-nyc -and-d-c-suburb; and Samuels, "Is Big Tech Merging."

12. Derysh, Igor, "Despite Parler Backlash, Facebook Played Huge Role in Fueling Capitol Riot, Watchdogs Say." Salon.com, Jan. 16, 2021. salon.com/2021/01/16 /despite-parler-backlash-facebook-played-huge-role-in-fueling-capitol-riot -watchdogs-say.

13. "Representative Ocasio-Cortez Questions Mark Zuckerberg on Facebook Fact-Checking Policy." C-SPAN, Oct. 23, 2019. c-span.org/video/?c4824531 %2Frepresentative-ocasio-cortez-questions-mark-zuckerberg-facebook-fact -checking-policy.

14. The Seasteading Institute, Oct. 1, 2021. seasteading.org.

Chapter Five: Embrace Your Inner Black Sheep

1. Faulkner, Donna. *Hitler: 1889–1933*. Boston: New Word City, 2015.

2. Peterson, Jordan B. "2017 Personality 20: Biology and Traits: Orderliness/Disgust/Conscientiousness." Uploaded on May 8, 2017, YouTube video, 1:34:32. youtube.com/watch?time_continue=5673&v=MBWyBdUYPgk&feature= emb_logo.

3. Murray, Damian R., Mark Schaller, and Peter Suedfeld. "Pathogens and Politics: Further Evidence That Parasite Prevalence Predicts Authoritarianism." *PLoS ONE* 8, no. 5 (May 2013): e62275. https://doi.org/10.1371/journal.pone .0062275.

4. Peterson, "Orderliness/Disgust/Conscientiousness."

5. Murray, Damian R., et al., "Pathogens and Politics."

6. Troianovski, Anton. "Not Just a Crisis: Coronavirus Is a Test for Putin's Security State." *The New York Times.* Mar. 19, 2020. nytimes.com/2020/03/19 /world/europe/coronavirus-russia-putin.html.

7. Kramer, Andrew E. "Putin Proposes Constitutional Ban on Gay Marriage." *The New York Times,* Mar. 3, 2020. nytimes.com/2020/03/03/world/europe/pu tin-proposes-constitutional-ban-on-gay-marriage.html.

8. Troianovski, Anton. "Not Just a Crisis: Coronavirus Is a Test for Putin's Security State." *The New York Times*, April 10, 2020. nytimes.com/2020/03/19 /world/europe/coronavirus-russia-putin.html.

9. Dixon, Robyn. "In Russia, Facial Surveillance and Threat of Prison Being Used to Make Coronavirus Quarantines Stick." *The Washington Post*, Mar. 25, 2020 .washingtonpost.com/world/europe/in-russia-facial-surveillance-and -risk-of-jail-seek-to-make-coronavirus-quarantines-stick/2020/03/24 /a590c7e8-6dbf-11ea-a156-0048b62cdb51_story.html.

10. Ritz, Erica. "The Reason Glenn Beck 'Cried All Day' after Receiving This Incredible Historical Document." *Blaze Media*, June 4, 2015. theblaze.com/news /2015/06/04/the-reason-glenn-beck-cried-all-day-after-receiving-this -incredible-historical-document.

11. Chan, Sewell. "71 Years after He Vanished, Raoul Wallenberg Is Declared Dead." *The New York Times,* Oct. 31, 2016. nytimes.com/2016/11/01/world/eu rope/71-years-after-he-vanished-raoul-wallenberg-is-declared-dead .html#:~:text=The%20official%20Soviet%20account%2C%20issued,of% 20the%20K.G.B.%20in%20Moscow.

12. "Rand Paul: Fauci Has Been Participating in Mask 'Theater' for Months." Fox Business. Uploaded on May 19, 2021, "Show Clips" video, 8:14. video.foxbusi ness.com/v/6255048369001#sp=show-clips.

13. McLeod, Saul. "Solomon Asch—Conformity Experiment." *Simply Psychology,* Dec. 28, 2018. simplypsychology.org/asch-conformity.html.

14. McLeod, "Solomon Asch—Conformity Experiment."

15. Campbell-Meiklejohn, Daniel K., et al. "Structure of Orbitofrontal Cortex Predicts Social Influence." *Current Biology* 22, no. 4 (Feb. 2012): R123–24. https:// doi.org/10.1016/j.cub.2012.01.012.

16. "Turkish Sheep Die in 'Mass Jump.'" BBC News (London). July 8, 2005. news .bbc.co.uk/2/hi/europe/4665511.stm.

17. "San Francisco Hair Salon Owner in Feud with Nancy Pelosi Talks to Tucker." Fox Business. Uploaded on 3 Sept. 3, 2020, "Show Clips" video, 4:38. video .foxnews.com/v/6187190778001.

Chapter Six: You Don't Need a Bunker (But You Do Need a Plan)

1. McGroarty, Beth. "Physical Activity Is an $828 Billion Market—To Reach $1.1 Trillion+ by 2023." Global Wellness Institute, Oct. 15, 2019. globalwellnessinstitute.org/press-room/press-releases/physical-activity-billion-market.

2. "World Population Is Getting Fatter." CBS News, May 29, 2014. cbsnews.com/news/world-population-is-getting-fatter-global-obesity-rates-rise.

3. "Skin Conditions by the Numbers: Acne." American Academy of Dermatology Association, 2013. aad.org/media/stats-numbers.

4. Hedegaard, Holly, Sally C. Curtin, and Margaret Warner. "Suicide Rates in the United States Continue to Increase." National Center for Health Statistics Data Brief No. 309, June 2018, cdc.gov/nchs/products/databriefs/db309.htm.

5. "First-Time Gun Buyers Grow to Nearly 5 Million in 2020." National Shooting Sports Foundation, Aug. 24, 2020. nssf.org/first-time-gun-buyers-grow-to-nearly-5-million-in-2020.

6. Van Sant, Will. "Gun Sales Have Hit Record Highs. Will It Change How Americans Vote?" *The Trace*, Aug. 22, 2020. thetrace.org/2020/08/do-gun-owners-vote-republican.

7. Ogg, Jon C. "Industries Making the Most Money on Doomsday Preppers." 24/WallStreet, 247wallst.com/special-report/2013/08/19/industries-making-the-most-money-on-doomsday-preppers/#ixzz2cQhAFgZU.

8. Laycock, Richard, and Catherine Choi. "Doomsday Prepper Statistics." Finder, Feb. 18, 2021. finder.com/doomsday-prepper-statistics.

9. Emerson, Ralph Waldo. "The Project Gutenberg EBook of Essays: Self-Reliance." Project Gutenberg. gutenberg.org/files/16643/16643-h/16643-h.htm#Footnote_165_165.

10. Emerson, "Project Gutenberg: Self-Reliance."

11. So, Adrienne. "Segway Is Bringing the Hoverchairs from *WALL-E* to Life." *Wired*, Jan. 3, 2020. wired.com/story/segway-bringing-hoverchairs-wall-e-life.

12. Powell, Michael. "In 9/11 Chaos, Giuliani Forged a Lasting Image." *The New York Times*, Sept. 21, 2007. nytimes.com/2007/09/21/us/politics/21giuliani.html.

13. Span, Paula. "Tragedy Brings Out Giuliani's Finest Hour." *South Florida Sun-Sentinel*, Sept. 15, 2001. sun-sentinel.com/news/fl-xpm-2001-09-15-01091 40810-story.html.

Chapter Seven: Capitalism > Socialism

1. Bergin, Brigid. "Crime Is the Key Issue in New York City Mayor's Race." NPR's *All Things Considered*, June 11, 2021. npr.org/2021/06/11/1005572002/crime -is-the-key-issue-in-new-york-city-mayors-race.

2. Lindbeck, Assar. *The Political Economy of the New Left: An Outsider's View.* New York: Harper and Row, 1972: 39.

3. Sowell, Thomas. *Basic Economics: A Citizen's Guide to the Economy.* New York: Basic Books, 2000.

4. Jennings, Tom. "Thomas Sowell: Common Sense in a Senseless World." Free to Choose Network, 2020. freetochoosenetwork.org/programs/thomas_sowell /credits.php.

5. Sowell, Thomas. "Depending on Dependency." Creators, Sept. 9, 2012. creators .com/read/thomas-sowell/09/12/depending-on-dependency.

6. Sowell, Thomas. "Blame the Welfare State, Not Racism, for Poor Blacks' Problems: Thomas Sowell." *PennLive Patriot-News*, May 7, 2015. pennlive.com /opinion/2015/05/poor_blacks_looking_for_someon.html.

7. Sheffield, Rachel, and Robert Rector. "The War on Poverty after 50 Years." The Heritage Foundation, Sept. 15, 2014. heritage.org/poverty-and-inequality/re port/the-war-poverty-after-50-years.

8. Creamer, John. "Inequalities Persist Despite Decline in Poverty for All Major Race and Hispanic Origin Groups." US Census Bureau, Sept.15, 2020. census .gov/library/stories/2020/09/poverty-rates-for-blacks-and-hispanics -reached-historic-lows-in-2019.html.

9. Council of Economic Advisors. "Incomes Hit a Record High and Poverty Reached a Record Low in 2019." WhiteHouse.gov, Sept. 15, 2020. trumpwhite house.archives.gov/articles/incomes-hit-record-high-poverty-reached -record-low-2019.

10. Semega, Jessica, et al. "Income and Poverty in the United States: 2019." Current Population Report P60–270, US Census Bureau, Sept. 15, 2020. census .gov/library/publications/2020/demo/p60-270.html.

11. American Express. "The 2019 State of Women-Owned Businesses Report." 2019. s1.q4cdn.com/692158879/files/doc_library/file/2019-state-of-women -owned-businesses-report.pdf.

12. Jennings, *Thomas Sowell: Common Sense.*

13. Havens, John J., and Paul G. Schervish. "Charitable Giving by State: New Methods and Measures for Geographic Giving Relative to Income." Paper presented at the 2015 Conference of the Association for Research on Nonprofit Organizations and Voluntary Action, Boston College, MA, Nov. 19, 2015. philanthropy.iupui.edu/doc/academics/philanthropy-research-workshop /prw170321.pdf.

14. Ayn Rand Archives. "Capitalism: The Unknown Ideal." AynRand.org, Oct. 4, 2021. aynrand.org/novels/capitalism-the-unknown-ideal.

15. Rand, Ayn. *Atlas Shrugged* (35th anniversary ed.), (New York: Dutton, 1992). "About the Author" in Rand 1992, pp. 1170–71.

16. Ayn Rand Archives, "Capitalism: the Unknown Ideal."

17. Davis, Clark. "Ayn Rand Studies on Campus, Courtesy of BB&T." NPR's *Morning Edition*, May 6, 2008. npr.org/templates/story/story.php?storyId=90104091.

18. "The Financial Crisis and the Free Market Cure: A Conversation with John A. Allison." *The Federalist Society*, Nov. 5, 2013. fedsoc.org/commentary/publica tions/the-financial-crisis-and-the-free-market-cure-a-conversation-with -john-a-allison.

19. Svanberg, Carl. "John Allison's Unconventional Wisdom about the Financial Crisis." *The Undercurrent*, Dec. 14, 2012. theundercurrent.org/john-allisons -unconventional-wisdom-about-the-financial-crisis.

Chapter Eight: The Eighteenth-Century Lesbian Poetry Trap

1. Cho, Mikael. "Why We Should Kill the 40-Hour Workweek." Observer Media, Mar. 24, 2017. observer.com/2017/03/kill-the-40-hour-work-week-productiv ity-office-culture-happiness/#.

2. "Surprising Working from Home Productivity Statistics (2021)." Apollo Technical, June 2, 2021. apollotechnical.com/working-from-home-productivity -statistics.

3. "Moving Beyond Remote: Workplace Transformation in the Wake of Covid-19." *Slack Collaboration* (blog), *Slack Technologies*, Oct. 7, 2020. slack.com/blog /collaboration/workplace-transformation-in-the-wake-of-covid-19.

4. "State of Remote Work 2019." Owl Labs, 2019. resources.owllabs.com/state-of -remote-work/2019.

5. Apollo Technical, "Working from Home (2021)."

6. Carney, Brian, and Isaac Getz. "Give Your Team the Freedom to Do the Work They Think Matters Most." *Harvard Business Review,* Sept. 10, 2018. hbr.org /2018/09/give-your-team-the-freedom-to-do-the-work-they-think-matters -most.

7. Federal Reserve Bank of New York, Economic Research. "The Labor Market for Recent College Graduates: Unemployment." *Unemployment Rates for College Graduates and Other Groups,* May 21, 2021, unnumbered chart. newyorkfed .org/research/college-labor-market/college-labor-market_unemployment .html.

8. "Thiel: College Diploma Is a Dunce Hat." CNN, Sept. 17, 2014. cnn.com/videos /bestoftv/2014/09/17/erin-intv-peter-thiel-on-college-education.cnn.

9. Juang, Mike. "A Secret Many Small-Business Owners Share with Mark Zuckerberg." CNBC.com, July 19, 2017. cnbc.com/2017/07/19/survey-shows-majority -of-business-owners-lack-college-degree.html.

Chapter Nine: Be a Hero, Not a Comrade

1. Abrams, Samuel J. "Family and Individualism: A New View of the American Dream." American Enterprise Institute, Apr. 24, 2019. aei.org/politics-and -public-opinion/family-and-individualism-a-new-view-of-the-american -dream.

2. Steinbuch, Yaron. "Black Lives Matter Co-Founder Describes Herself as 'Trained Marxist.'" *New York Post,* June 25, 2020. nypost.com/2020/06/25 /blm-co-founder-describes-herself-as-trained-marxist.

3. Leonardi, Anthony. "Black Lives Matter 'What We Believe' Page That Includes Disrupting 'Nuclear Family Structure' Removed from Website." *The Washington Examiner*, Sept. 21, 2020. washingtonexaminer.com/news/black-lives -matter-what-we-believe-page-that-includes-disrupting-nuclear-family -structure-removed-from-website.

4. "404 Not Found." Black Lives Matter, Oct. 5, 2021. blacklivesmatter.com/what -we-believe/?__cf_chl_jschl_tk__.

5. Whyte, Martin King, Wang Feng, and Yong Cai. "Challenging Myths About China's One-Child Policy." National Center for Biotechnology Information, PubMed Central, Aug. 20, 2019. ncbi.nlm.nih.gov/pmc/articles/PMC670 1844/#FN8.

6. Fallows, James. "The Reinvention of America." *The Atlantic*, Apr. 23, 2018. the atlantic.com/magazine/archive/2018/05/reinventing-america/556856.

Index